LAW AND FINANCE IN RETIRE...

About the Author

John Costello is head of the private client department of Eugene F. Collins, Solicitors. He has practised in wills, administration of estates, trusts, tax planning, wards of court, powers of attorney and other legal issues affecting the older person, for nearly twenty years. He is also practising in family law and acts for many clients applying for a divorce.

He is a council member of the Law Society of Ireland and outgoing Chairman of the Law Society Committee on Probate and Taxation. He is Vice-Chairman of the Law Society Law Reform Committee and a member of the Law Society Committee on Mental Health and Disability. He is a former committee member of the Commission on the Status of People with Disabilities.

LAW AND FINANCE IN RETIREMENT

John Costello

Solicitor
Eugene F. Collins

BLACKHALL
Publishing

This book was typeset by Gough Typesetting Services for

BLACKHALL PUBLISHING
26 Eustace Street
Dublin 2
Ireland

e-mail: blackhall@eircom.net
www.blackhallpublishing.com

ISBN: 1 901657 80 9

A catalogue record for this book is
available from the British Library.

Printed in Ireland by
Betaprint Ltd

Contents

Preface xi
Acknowledgments xiii
Foreword xv

1. **Wills and Tax** 1
   Definition of a Will 1
   What Are the Requirements for a Valid Will? 1
   Why Make a Will? 1
   Why Go to a Solicitor? 2
   What Will it Cost? 2
   Background Information for Making a Will 3
   Probate Tax 9
   Capital Acquisitions Tax 11
   Gift/Inheritance Tax: Questions and Answers 12
   Conclusion 16

2. **Legal Issues which Arise after a Person Dies** 17
   Funeral Arrangements 17
   Trustees 20
   Procedure to Take Out a Grant of Probate 21
   Procedure to Take Out Letters of Administration Intestate 23
   After the Grant of Probate Issues 24
   Rights of a Surviving Spouse 25
   Charitable Bequests 26
   Obligations under Social Welfare Legislation 26
   Joint Bank Accounts 27
   Assets outside Ireland 27
   Legal Rights of Children 28
   Statutory Notice to Creditors 28
   Finalising the Administration of the Estate 29
   Legal Fees 29

3.   **Legal Arrangements for Managing Financial Affairs
     when an Older Person Becomes Unwell** 31
     Joint Bank Accounts 31
     Agency Arrangements for Social Welfare Payments 32
     Powers of Attorney 34
     Enduring Powers of Attorney 36
     Additional Duties of an Attorney under an EPA 42
     Wards of Court 43
     Trusts 47
     Types of Trusts 48
     Covenants 49
     References 50

4.   **A Guide to Occupational and Personal Pensions** 51
     A Guide to Pensions 51
     Occupational Pensions 52
     Contributions and Benefits that Apply to
        Occupational Schemes 52
     Defined Benefit Schemes and Defined Contribution Schemes ... 54
     Personal Pensions 57
     Personal Pension Plans: Changes Introduced in the
        Finance Act 1999 57
     Specific Provisions 58
     Pensions Board 59
     Further Information 60

5.   **State and Health Board Income Support for Older or
     Retired People** 61
     Introduction 61
     Retirement Pension 63
     Old Age Contributory Pension 64
     Pension Arrangements for the Self-Employed 66
     Old Age Non-Contributory Pension 67
     Pre-Retirement Allowance 71
     EU Farm Retirement Scheme 71
     Widows'/Widowers' Contributory Pension 73
     Widows'/Widowers' Non-Contributory Pension 73
     Payments Arising from a Death 74
     Additional Payments 75
     Free Schemes 78
     Free Travel 78

Free Electricity Allowance 80
Free Natural Gas Allowance 81
Free Bottled Gas Refill Allowance 82
Free Electricity (Group Account) Allowance 82
Free Telephone Rental Allowance 83
Fuel Allowance 84
Medical Card 84
Drugs Payment Scheme 85
Scheme of Community Support for Older People 85
References 86
Maximum Weekly Increases from May 2000 — Tables 1–3 87
Useful Addresses 90

6. **Community and Residential Care** 95
    Community Care Services 95
    Residential Care 96
    Nursing Home Options 96
    Choosing a Nursing Home 97
    The Regulation of Nursing Homes 99
    Code of Practice for Nursing Homes 100
    Nursing Home Subventions 104
    Financing Long-Term Residential Care 105
    List of Agencies that Assist with Queries Relating to
        Nursing Homes or Carers 107

7. **Savings and Investments** 108
    Introduction to Investments 108
    Purchasing Stocks and Shares on the Stock Exchange 112
    Investment Funds 113
    Investments under Certain Tax Incentive Schemes 117
    Summary 117

8. **Income Tax and Capital Gains Tax** 118
    Introduction 118
    Income Tax 119
    Allowances 120
    Lump Sum Payments on Redundancy/Retirement 127
    Refund of Deposit Interest Retention Tax 128
    How to Complain to the Revenue 129
    Capital Gains Tax 129
    Further Information 134

References 134
Table of Multipliers for Disposal 135
Tax Offices.. 136
Summary of Tax Allowances, Rates and Exemptions 137
1 December 1999 Budget changes 138

9.   **Separation and Divorce**.. 142
     Introduction.. 142
     Separation Agreements... 143
     Judicial Separation 144
     Divorce 145
     Orders for Judicial Separation/Divorce.................... 146
     Orders which the Court Can Make in Judicial Separation/
          Divorce Proceedings.. 146
     Tax Provisions 152
     First Consultation with a Solicitor 153
     Useful Addresses 153

10. **Medical Treatment** 157
     Consent to Treatment.. 157
     Ward of Court Case 159
     Advance Directives/Living Wills 161
     Sample Living Will... 162

11. **Enforcing Legal Rights Cheaply** 164
     Small Claims Court 164
     The Ombudsman.. 165
     The Information Commissioner 166
     Civil Legal Aid 168
     The Insurance Ombudsman of Ireland 169
     Insurance Information Service................................... 171
     Department of Enterprise, Trade and Employment.................. 171

Appendix
     List of Organisations Working for Older People 172
     Citizens' Information Centres 176
     Health Boards 182

Glossary 183

Index 193

For my wife Ita and children, Laura, Eleanor and Mark

Preface

Groucho Marx once said: "Anyone can get old. All you have to do is live long enough". Happily, many people who enjoyed the films of the Marx Brothers in the 1930s, are still enjoying the films which Hollywood produces today. This is because in Ireland, the average life expectancy is 72 years for males and 77 for females. When the Marx Brothers' films were first produced, the average life expectancy in Ireland was only about 58 years.

Demographics

In Ireland in 1996, there were approximately 414,000 people over the age of 65, i.e. 11 per cent of the total population. Seventy-eight per cent live full independent lives, 17 per cent are cared for at home and 5 per cent are cared for in institutions. It is estimated that 5 per cent of Irish people over 65 suffer from some form of senile dementia and that there are more than 25,000 suffering from Alzheimer's Disease in Ireland at the present time. In 2011, there will be in excess of 520,000 people over the age of 65 years, i.e. approximately, 14.1 per cent of the population.

Income and Pensions

In 1995, nearly 95 per cent of people aged over 66 received Social Welfare pensions. Almost 23 per cent received an Occupational Pension from a previous employer. Over the past twenty years, the income of older people has improved significantly with increased pension levels. However, there are still many groups of vulnerable older people in poverty, living alone or with disabilities.

Emerging Problems

From my experience of twenty years as a solicitor dealing with many older clients, the greatest problem facing families is finding proper care for older relations when required, either in their own homes or in residential care. Coupled with these practical problems, is the lack of awareness generally, as to what community care services and what State and health board income support is available for older people. Finally, there are the legal problems which arise when an older person's physical or mental health deteriorates and the decision as to what legal safeguards should be taken in this situation. Many older people can be in a very vulnerable position when their health deteriorates and sometimes the present laws are inadequate to deal with all the problems which emerge.

Law Reform

Many problems with older clients emerge when they have lost the capacity to make decisions or to care for themselves. For example, if an older person is at risk of abuse or exploitation, a health board should be able to place this older person in the care of a relative, health board or a voluntary agency, as directed by a court.

The wards of court procedures should be simplified in certain cases and fast track procedures should apply for emergencies. Finally, the law should be reviewed regarding how healthcare decisions are made when an older person cannot give consent to medical treatment. In June 1997, Singapore opened a special court called "The Tribunal for the Maintenance of Persons", a place where senior citizens can press legal claims against their children for not taking proper care of them. Would similar legislation ever be passed in Ireland or the EU?

Conclusion

This book is aimed at providing some useful information on some of the most common legal, taxation, social welfare, pension, family, savings and healthcare matters relevant to older people. It is not possible to cover every issue which could arise, but hopefully, most of the important questions relating to these issues have been dealt with.

Mark Twain once said: "Life would be infinitely happier if one could only be born at the age of 80 and gradually approach 18". My answer is that if we can think like an 18 year old, with the wisdom of an 80 year old, we can enjoy the next millennium.

Acknowledgements

1999 was the UN International Year of the Older Person. Inspired by this event, I spent many evenings in my study writing this book. My wife Ita and my children Laura, Eleanor and Mark, did not always have my unfailing attention during this year. I thank them for their patience and encouragement when I undertook this enterprise. I am happy to report, that for me at any rate, 2000 will be the year of the family.

I would like to thank my publisher Gerard O'Connor for suggesting that I write this book and for his optimism that it would eventually see the light of day.

I would, in particular, like to thank my secretary Sharon Carroll who typed every word of this book. Her enormous hard work, dedication and enthusiasm in assisting me with this book is immensely appreciated and without her contribution, this book would never have been completed.

Finally, I would like to thank professional colleagues who assisted me in finalising certain chapters. Ann McKenna, Solicitor, gave me excellent suggestions for my chapter on wills. Eugene Davy, Solicitor, provided his expertise in finalising the chapter on divorce and separation. Basil D'Arcy of Goodbody Stockbrokers, gave me very helpful suggestions in the area of savings and investments. My brother David and Mary Hutch, Solicitor with the Pensions Board, gave me some of their expertise on pensions. John Long of the National Social Services Board was a mine of information on Social Welfare benefits. Finally, Ann O'Dwyer of the Retirement Association of Home Information Service Ltd. gave me invaluable information on nursing homes. To all these people, I say a very sincere thank you.

Foreword

Somebody once wrote that 'old age is the most unexpected of all things that can happen to a man'. While this may have been true in the past, old age is something to which we can all now, thankfully, look forward. But it is also something for which we must plan. This book provides essential information which will assist us all in that task.

As Minister with responsibility for social affairs, I am delighted that the needs of our retired people have been widely recognised and that steps have been taken to improve the position of older people in relation to a wide range of services.

I am very pleased to welcome this important contribution to the information available to older people with particular reference to legal and financial issues. It will not, of course, just be of great benefit to older people themselves and their families but will be essential reading for all those of us who work with and for older people.

John Costello is particularly well qualified to have written this book. He is one of – if not the – leading expert in this area. He has produced a text which is both clearly written and comprehensive. All those who have worked in this area will recognise his achievement.

I thoroughly commend this book and recommend it to a wide audience.

Dermot Ahern TD
Minister for Social, Community and Family Affairs.

Chapter One

Wills and Tax

DEFINITION OF A WILL

A will is a written document in which a person sets out legally binding wishes in relation to the distribution of a property after death. A person who makes a will is called a testator/testatrix. A person who dies without having made a will is deemed to have died intestate and the distribution of an intestate's assets is among the next of kin as set out in the Succession Act 1965.

WHAT ARE THE REQUIREMENTS FOR A VALID WILL?

A will must be in writing and must be signed by a testator/testatrix over the age of eighteen years. The testator must be of sound mind and sign the will in the presence of two witnesses who in turn, must sign the will in the testator's presence. If the testator is unable to sign the will then he/she can execute the will by making a mark. If a beneficiary or a spouse of a beneficiary witnesses a testator's will, then that witness cannot legally receive the benefit under the will. However, an executor, trustee or guardian can be a beneficiary under the will. If the testator marries after making a will, then the will is revoked automatically by marriage, unless the will is made in contemplation of the marriage.

WHY MAKE A WILL?

If you are married and die without making a will, leaving a spouse and children, your spouse inherits two-thirds of all you own (called your "estate") and your children inherit the remaining one-third. If the family home is solely in your name, your children could ask for one-third of its value, leaving financial problems for your surviving spouse. If you are single and die intestate, your estate is distributed among your next of kin, as set out in the Succession Act 1965. By making a will, you can avoid these problems and achieve the following:

- express your burial wishes and any other details concerning funeral arrangements or the disposal of your body
- save your next of kin or other beneficiaries substantial inheritance tax and/or probate tax
- appoint guardians for any children under the age of eighteen if yourself and your spouse die in an accident
- leave specific assets to specific children or beneficiaries and specify that certain beneficiaries can only inherit property on attaining the age of 21 or older
- make a precise provision for a beneficiary who may have a drink problem, a gambling problem, is irresponsible when it comes to money or who may suffer from a mental disability — in this situation, the will can set up a trust for the protection of such a beneficiary.

WHY GO TO A SOLICITOR?

You can draw up your own will or have it done by anyone you please, but it is best to go to a solicitor. This isn't just because of the necessity to use clear unambiguous language but also because a solicitor will:

- help you clarify your own ideas — your will needs to cater for a number of different eventualities and you may not have thought of all of them
- use legal expertise in preparing the will — it will involve a knowledge not only of the law of wills but also of the law of property, trusts, tax and perhaps other subjects as well
- ensure that the will is drafted in such a way so as to reduce the likelihood of it being challenged after your death.

Your will is probably the most important document you will ever sign and it must be right. The future well being of your family may depend on it — not only financially but also for a harmonious future, because a badly drawn up will can create lasting grievances.

WHAT WILL IT COST?

Solicitor's charges are likely to be small when weighed against the peace

of mind you gain (or from the tax savings that may be gained). Most solicitors should give you an idea of likely costs beforehand, and you could
get several quotes if you so wish. Your will should be tailored to your own
needs — there is really no such thing as a "standard will" and solicitors
cannot tell exactly what the costs will be until they know what is required.
Remember too, buying a will is not like buying a newspaper or a loaf of
bread, because you yourself can't really tell how good it is.

Charges must be reasonable and a solicitor is obliged to tell you the
cost of the will before you give instructions for the drafting of the will. A
solicitor in a legal aid centre may be able to draft your will for a nominal
amount if your income and savings are such that you qualify for legal aid.

BACKGROUND INFORMATION FOR MAKING A WILL

An Individual

Your solicitor will need to know a number of things about you. Some are
obvious — whether you are married, are contemplating marriage or were
previously married; whether you have young children or older ones, grandchildren and so on. Others may be less obvious. If you have foreign property, a foreign domicile, have made a foreign will or if you or your family
have interests under any existing trusts, you should communicate these
along with any other facts that could be relevant.

Your Estate

It is helpful to list the things you own with some indication of their value.
This might include a house or flat, any land or buildings, investments
(including money and shares, unit trusts in a bank or building society or a
post office account), furniture and jewellery. It should mention any life or
endowment insurance policies and pension entitlements and any existing
arrangements about what happens to them on your death.

Joint Ownership

If you are a co-owner (with your spouse or someone else) of your house or
flat or of any bank account, this should also be mentioned. If there is
money in a joint bank account with another person or persons, then it is
important to specify whether it is your intention that the monies in this
joint bank account would pass to the survivor(s) named in the account on
your death.

Executors and Trustees

In every will, an executor has to be appointed to carry out the wishes stated in the will. The executor must pay all the debts and liabilities that arise up to the date of death and that arise during the administration of the estate. If the will is very simple, one person could be appointed to act alone, e.g. your spouse, but it is usually better to appoint at least two people. You could make alternative appointments to cover the risk of an executor dying before you or being unable to act when the time comes. Other relations or friends can also be appointed as executors. It can also be useful to appoint a bank or professional people, such as solicitors or accountants, as executors where, for instance, the estate is complicated or there are complicated family circumstances. If professional persons or a bank are appointed executors or trustees they charge fees for acting.

Executors are also the persons primarily responsible for making the funeral arrangements for the deceased. However, in practice, the next of kin normally makes the arrangements, taking into account any wishes expressed by the deceased in the will.

Non-professional executors, although they can claim their expenses, are not paid for their work. You might consider leaving them something for acting on your behalf. Before you appoint them, you should also make sure that they are willing to act as executors.

Trustees

You may not wish your children to receive money directly, but may wish to put a sum of money in a trust for them until they reach the age of eighteen or older. As mentioned above, you may also wish to remember a beneficiary who has a drink problem, a gambling problem, is irresponsible when it comes to money or who has a disability. In any of these situations, you need to appoint trustees (who can also be the executors) who would hold the benefit on trust for the beneficiary until the beneficiary attains the age specified in the will or for the lifetime of the beneficiary, whichever is specified in the will. Normally, where there is a trust the will specifies that the trustees hold a specific fund or share and have the power to distribute that fund, at their discretion, when required by the beneficiary. The will should also specify how any undistributed part of the fund will be divided on the death of the beneficiary.

Appointment of Guardians

If you and your spouse were unfortunate enough to be killed in an accident, leaving behind children under the age of eighteen years, your relatives would have to apply to the court to have guardians appointed for your children. This can be avoided by naming guardians in your will. A guardian is the person you select to take over your role as parent in rearing your children under the age of eighteen years. Therefore, the guardians have a different role from the trustees who manage the fund or the property that is held for the benefit of the beneficiary. Nevertheless, guardians and trustees may be the same persons.

Legal Separation/Divorce

If you are legally separated or divorced from your spouse, by making a will you can minimise the legal entitlement of your spouse and help reduce legal problems at a later stage. If you are divorced, then the terms of the court order will determine whether your former spouse can challenge your will.

Rights of the Surviving Spouse

If you die testate, i.e. with a will, your spouse is legally entitled to one-third of your estate if you leave surviving children, or one half of your estate if you have no surviving children. The one-third share or one-half share is in addition to any joint property which the surviving spouse automatically inherits on your death.

Legal Separation

Separation itself does not extinguish succession rights. However, such rights may be extinguished or renounced under a separation agreement, judicial separation or can be precluded by a court order on divorce.

Divorce

In the case of divorce, a former spouse for whom proper provision has not been made during his/her lifetime may apply to court for relief within six months from the date of the Grant of Probate or Grant of Administration. Personal representatives are required to take reasonable steps to notify the former spouse. Such relief is not available to a former spouse who has remarried.

"Partner"

If not married to you, your "partner" will have no succession rights and will therefore be limited to whatever rights he/she may establish in contract (e.g. where he/she has financially contributed to the purchase of a property or whatever he/she is entitled to under your will).

Rights of the Surviving Children

A child, unlike a spouse, is not entitled to any specified share in a deceased parent's estate as of right. However, section 117 of the Succession Act 1965 allows a child to make an application to court where the child would like a share or greater share from his/her parent's estate than that provided under the will.

In order to succeed with such a claim, the court must be of the opinion that the testator has failed in his/her moral duty to make proper provision for the child in accordance with his/her means. In these circumstances, the court may order that such provision should be made for the child out of the estate as the court thinks "just". The court is obliged to consider the matter from the point of view of a prudent and just parent, and must take into account the position of each of the children of the testator and any other circumstances that the court considers to be of assistance in deciding what is as fair as possible to the child and to the other children.

Quite often an elderly parent may be cared for in their home for many years by an unmarried child. In this situation, the elderly parent may recognise this contribution of the child by leaving the house to that specific child. However, if other children in the family are not well off, it may be possible to reach a compromise so that all the children benefit, e.g. by leaving the house to the child still living at home, provided that that child pays a sum of money to each of the other children in the family when he/she inherits the house from the deceased parent.

If a parent dies intestate, i.e. without a will, the Succession Act 1965 stipulates the share which the next of kin receive. A child, in this situation, cannot apply to court for a greater share than that set out in the Succession Act.

Children Born outside Marriage

The position of non-marital children was altered by the Status of Children Act 1987. This states that children born outside of marriage have equal rights with those born inside the institution of marriage. The act essentially states that the relationship between every person and his/her father or mother (or either of them) shall, unless the contrary intention appears, be determined irrespective of whether his/her mother and father are or have been married to each other, and all other relationships will be determined accordingly.

If a testator wishes to make a proper provision for "all my children or grandchildren in equal shares", he must be advised that this will automatically include both marital and non-marital children and grandchildren, unless the contrary intention appears. If the testator does not wish to benefit any relations born outside of marriage, then the will can provide that the provisions of the Status of Children Act 1987 do not apply.

Joint Property

Lands or residence: if you own land or a residence jointly with another person, it is important that the solicitor preparing your will is informed whether the joint ownership is a joint tenancy or a tenancy in common. If the joint ownership is a joint tenancy, then the surviving owner will automatically inherit your share of the property on your death. Nevertheless, if the joint ownership is a tenancy in common, then you can leave your share to any beneficiary or beneficiaries under your will and the surviving joint owner will not have any automatic legal entitlement to your share of the property.

When making your will in such circumstances, the solicitor should seek a copy of your title deeds pertaining to the property in this situation.

Joint bank accounts: if you have a joint bank account with another person, the question can arise on your death as to who is entitled to the beneficial ownership of the monies in the joint account. Different legal considerations apply to determine this question, depending on the intention of the parties, the extent to which they each contributed to the account and the terms of their contract with the bank. For example, where the contract with your bank is that the money should be payable on your death to the survivor in the account, then no difficulty arises if this specific instruction is given to the bank when you open the account.

Where the surviving owner of the joint bank account is the surviving spouse or surviving child, then unless a contrary intention is shown, the courts normally decide that all the monies in the joint bank account are to pass to the surviving spouse or surviving child. However, if the joint owners of the bank account are not spouses or children, the courts have held that all the monies in the joint account on the death of one party form part of the deceased's estate where the deceased had provided the funds to open the account. In these cases, the courts have a discretion which they have often automatically exercised, to presume that the money is held by the surviving joint owner on trust for the deceased's estate i.e. the monies are distributed in accordance with the deceased's will or to the deceased's closest next-of-kin if there is no will.

Yet, in a recent judgment of the Supreme Court *(Lynch* v. *Burke,* November 1995*),* the Supreme Court held that because of the facts in that case and because of the intention of the deceased joint owner, it was only correct that the funds in the joint account should pass absolutely to the surviving joint owner in the account, namely, a niece of the deceased.

As a result of this decision, it is very important that when making a will, a testator should leave written instructions as to who is to inherit any money in a joint bank account on their death. The testator's intentions should also be made clear to the second person named in the account and if possible referred to in the will.

Letter of Wishes

Where the will creates a trust for one or more beneficiaries, it is useful for the testator to execute a letter of wishes addressed to the trustees. This is a letter giving guidelines to the trustees as to how they might operate the trust for the benefit of the beneficiaries, e.g. when to distribute assets to each beneficiary and when to terminate the trust if the will does not specify this. The letter of wishes is not a legally binding document but is morally binding on the trustees who would normally follow its direction. The trustees are not obliged to show a copy of the letter of wishes to the beneficiaries.

Changing the Will

It is wise to reconsider your will every few years with your solicitor, just to make sure that there have been no changes in your own circumstances, those of the beneficiaries, or in the law or tax system, which makes alterations desirable.

Simple alterations to a will may be made by codicil (a document executed in the same way, which makes minor changes to the will but which leaves most of it intact). If the alterations are extensive, it is better to have a new will drawn up. In particular, if you are revoking a legacy in your existing will, it is preferable to make a new will rather than a codicil. If you simply revoked a legacy in a codicil, then after probate, when the will and codicil is a public document, the beneficiary would be able to see that he/she was once left a legacy that was subsequently revoked. However, if the legacy is revoked in a later will, only the last will is a public document after the grant of probate issues and no one is entitled to see any earlier wills the testator may have made. If a testator makes a new will, then any earlier will or wills can only be destroyed in the presence and on the instructions of the testator or by the testator personally.

PROBATE TAX

Property Liable to Probate Tax

A probate tax of 2 per cent must be paid on the value of the property of all persons dying after 17 June 1993. The extent to which an estate is taxable depends on the domicile of the deceased. If the deceased is domiciled in the State, all assets wherever located, are subject to probate tax (apart from those specifically exempted). If the deceased is not domiciled in the State, only assets situated in the State are liable to the tax.

Debts owing at the time of death (and funeral expenses) can be deducted in arriving at the net value of the assets that are subject to probate tax.

Any property which is inherited absolutely by a surviving spouse is exempt from probate tax.

When the Tax Is Payable

The tax must be paid within nine months of the date of death. However, the revenue has the power to postpone the tax where there are insufficient liquid assets to pay it. After nine months, interest is payable on the tax at 12 per cent per annum, if still outstanding.

Certain government stocks can be used to pay the tax. The revenue will accept these stocks at their nominal value in payment of probate tax, even if their market value on the Stock Exchange is then lower.

In addition, the proceeds of section 60 Life Policies can be utilised to pay probate tax. These are life policies taken out specifically to pay inheritance tax on the death of the deceased.

Property Exempt from ProbateTax

This includes:

- property inherited absolutely by a surviving spouse
- the family home where a dependent child or dependent relative is residing in the house and his/her annual income does not exceed £4,848 (for the tax year 1999/2000). (Note: the family home exemption includes grounds of up to one acre and "normal" furniture and household effects)
- superannuation benefits, e.g. pension benefits
- property left to charity
- joint property
- estates less than £10,000 (excluding the family home if it is already exempt). The £10,000 will be indexed each year. For 1999, it amounted to £11,250. In respect of deaths on or after 1 December 1999, the exemption threshold of £11,250 is increased to £40,000 (provided for in the Finance Bill 2000)
- property transferred to a trust during the lifetime of the deceased
- agricultural property inherited on a death — only 70 per cent of the full market value of the property is subject to the probate tax.

A dependent child is a child who has not attained the age of eighteen years, or is receiving full-time education.

A dependent relative is, in relation to an individual, a relative of the individual or of the wife or husband of the individual, who is incapacitated through old age or infirmity and unable to maintain himself/herself, or the widowed mother (whether or not she is incapacitated) of the individual or of the wife or husband of the individual.

Special Relief on the Death of a Surviving Spouse

There is no probate tax payable if a surviving spouse dies within one year of the other spouse. Nevertheless, if the surviving spouse dies within five years of the other spouse and leaves a dependent child, then no probate tax will be payable either.

Avoidance of Probate Tax

The proceeds of section 60 Life Policies and certain government stocks may be used to discharge the tax. The most straightforward way of avoiding the probate tax is by placing assets in joint names. However, if property is placed in the joint names of parties other than spouses, there could be a liability to stamp duty, gift tax and capital gains tax. Tax advice is required before transferring property into joint names. For example, brothers and sisters could place property in joint names to avoid the probate tax.

CAPITAL ACQUISITIONS TAX

The Finance Bill 2000 (published on 10 February 2000) introduced a new Family Home Relief and new Residence Rules as described below. The details are subject to the normal legislative process and to the enactment of the necessary legislation in the Finance Act 2000.

Family Home Relief

For gifts or inheritances of a dwellinghouse taken on or after 1 December 1999, CAT will no longer apply provided that:

- it is the principal private residence of the disponer and/or the recipient

- the recipient has been living in the house for the three years prior to the transfer

- the recipient does not have an interest in any other house and

- the recipient must occupy the dwellinghouse as his or her only or main residence for six years after the gift/inheritance (this condition does not apply if the recipient is over 55 at the date of the gift/inheritance or dies before the six year period expires).

If the dwellinghouse has been acquired either directly or indirectly after a previous property was sold, the relief applies if the recipient has continuously occupied both properties as his/her own and main residence for a total period of three out of the four years prior to the date of the gift or inheritance.

The exemption will not be withdrawn if the recipient has to leave the dwellinghouse within the six-year period to receive long-term medical care in a hospital, nursing home or convalescent home or as a result of a condition being imposed by an employer on a recipient to reside elsewhere.

The exemption will be withdrawn if the recipient sells or otherwise disposes of dwellinghouse within the relevant six-year period, unless the sale or disposal is as a result of the recipient requiring long-term medical care in a hospital, nursing home or convalescent home.

Replacement of Domicile Rule by Resident/Ordinarily Resident Rules

Gifts or inheritances of non-Irish situated property, taken on or after 1 December 1999, will be liable to tax where either the disponer (i.e. the person disposing of the property by gift or will) or beneficiary is resident or ordinarily resident in the State. These new rules will not apply for gifts or inheritances taken under a trust or settlement existing on the 1 December 1999 (which will be subject to the old rules). Any property situated in the State is subject to the Irish Capital Acquisitions Tax Rules.

A foreign domiciled person will not be considered to be resident or ordinarily resident in the State until 1 December 2004 and then only if he or she has been resident in the State for the five consecutive tax years preceding the gift or inheritance.

GIFT/INHERITANCE TAX: QUESTIONS AND ANSWERS

Q: How much gift tax or inheritance tax is payable by a beneficiary under a will?

A: The only gift or inheritance that is free from tax is one between a husband and a wife or vice versa. If other relations/beneficiaries receive a gift or inheritance (under a will), the following amounts from 1 December 1999 (called "threshold amounts" adjusted each year for inflation) are free of gift tax or inheritance tax (as announced in the Budget of 1 December 1999):

• for a son, daughter or parent: £300,000 (Group 1)

• for a sister, brother, nephew, niece, grandchild, great-grandchild: £30,000 (Group 2)

• for any other relation or no relation (*i.e.* a stranger): £15,000 (Group 3).

The new thresholds will be indexed from 1 January 2001, i.e. they will be increased in line with the consumer price index.

All gifts and inheritances received after 2 December 1988 are aggregated together when calculating the tax you owe on your latest gift or inheritance, provided the prior gifts or inheritances are within the same group (1, 2 or 3) as the latest gift or inheritance.

Q: What are the rates of gift tax or inheritance tax?

A: In respect of inheritances or gifts received after 1 December 1999 (as announced in the Budget), a single 20 per cent rate of tax replaces the rates of 30 per cent and 40 per cent which applied previously.

Amount of Inheritance	Tax Rate Percentage
Up to threshold amount	Nil
Balance	20 per cent

Q: How can I reduce the impact of inheritance tax?

A: By making a will, you can distribute your assets to several members of your family to minimise the overall inheritance tax liability. Alternatively, you can leave a life interest under your will to a beneficiary (as opposed to an absolute interest). With a life interest, the beneficiary only receives the annual income from the legacy, which is invested for the duration of the lifetime of the beneficiary. The beneficiary is not entitled to any lump sum capital payments from the monies invested on his/her behalf. The advantage of a life interest is that it substantially reduces the inheritance tax liability. The inheritance tax payable on a life interest depends on the age of the beneficiary when he/she receives the benefit.

Q: Can proceeds of a life policy be used to cover inheritance tax payable by a beneficiary under my will?

A: Section 60 of the Finance Act 1985 introduced a provision making the proceeds of a life assurance policy exempt from inheritance tax when it is specifically set aside to pay for the inheritance tax liability of one or more beneficiaries. These life assurance policies, known as "Section 60" policies, are a very cost effective way of minimising or avoiding an inheritance tax liability.

Q: Does a lifetime gift reduce the tax liability of a beneficiary?

A: No. The Finance Bill 2000 provided that from 1 December 2000, both gifts and inheritances are to be taxed at 20 per cent, if they are not below the tax thresholds. The amount of the gift or inheritance exceeding the tax threshold is taxed at 20 per cent.

Q: If I have agricultural property, is there any special relief from gift or inheritance tax?

A: Yes. In calculating the taxable value of a gift or inheritance of agricultural property, the market value of the property is reduced substantially. There are a number of conditions attached to this relief:

1. Agricultural property includes agricultural land, woodlands, farmhouses and buildings, farm machinery, livestock and bloodstock.

2. The reduction is only allowed where the beneficiary is a "farmer". The definition of a farmer in this instance is someone who can show that at least 80 per cent of his assets after receiving the gift or inheritance consists of agricultural property.

3. The agricultural relief will be lost if the beneficiary sells the agricultural property within six years of receiving it unless it is replaced within a year by other agricultural property. In that event, the gift or inheritance tax is assessed under the normal rules and the tax originally saved has to be repaid to the Revenue.

4. Where there is a gift or inheritance of agricultural property the value of the agricultural property is reduced by 90 per cent.

Q: When does inheritance tax or gift tax need to be paid?

A: The tax must be paid within four months of receiving the inheritance/ gift or being deemed to have received the inheritance, i.e. when the grant of probate issues. Interest is charged at a rate of 12 per cent per annum on any overdue tax.

Q: If I own a business is there any special relief from gift or inheritance tax?

A: Yes. In calculating the taxable value of a gift or inheritance of certain business properties, the market value of the property is reduced by 90 per cent. The relief applies to business property as defined. This includes:

• property consisting of a business or an interest in a business

• unquoted shares or securities of an Irish company subject to the condition that:

   (a) the beneficiary holds at least 25 per cent of the voting rights
   or
   (b) the beneficiary holds at least 10 per cent of the issued capital of the company and the company is controlled by the beneficiary and his/ her relatives
   or
   (c) the beneficiary holds at least 10 per cent of the issued capital of the

company and has worked full-time in the company for five years prior to the gift or inheritance.

The relief does not apply to a business wholly or mainly dealing in land, shares, securities or currencies, or to making or holding investments.

In order to qualify for the relief the relevant business property must have been owned by the disponer or his/her spouse for at least five years prior to a gift and for at least two years prior to an inheritance under a will.

The relief may be lost if the beneficiary sells the business property within six years of receiving it and it is not replaced within a year by another relevant business property.

Q: Are there any reliefs for nephews/nieces?

A: If the beneficiary is a nephew or niece who worked full-time in the business for five years and you leave the business to him/her, then he/she will be entitled to the same tax-free threshold as a son or daughter in relation to that property.

Q: Are there any special tax implications with discretionary trusts?

A: A discretionary trust is useful when the person making the will wants to benefit a wide group of people (e.g. to include a potential issue not yet born) and would like to provide for some flexibility as to who should benefit or the amount they should be given. It can also be used if the beneficiary has a mental disability, has a drink or gambling problem or is merely irresponsible with money.

Discretionary trusts are liable to a once-off tax of 6 per cent on the death of the person creating the trust, once his/her spouse and all their children are over the age of 21. There may be a refund of 3 per cent of the tax if the trust fund is distributed fully within five years. There is a further payment of 1 per cent due each year following the payment of the 6 per cent (except for the first year). There is no discretionary trust tax payable where the beneficiary has a disability.

Q: Do the particular assets which I own affect the amount of inheritance tax that may be payable by the beneficiaries under my will?

A: If you own assets located in the United Kingdom (including UK stocks and shares), then UK inheritance tax may be payable on these assets. There is no UK inheritance tax if these assets are inherited by a surviving spouse.

If you hold certain government stocks at the date of your death, any one or more beneficiaries can use these government stocks to pay inherit-

ance tax. The Revenue will accept these in payment of inheritance tax at
their nominal value, even if their market value on the Stock Exchange is
lower. They must be transferred directly to the Revenue, otherwise the
benefit is lost.

If you have a beneficiary who is neither resident nor domiciled in the
Republic of Ireland, then you can leave certain government stocks, either
during your lifetime or under your will, to this beneficiary absolutely free
of tax. However, there are requirements regarding the period of time these
stocks must be held.

CONCLUSION

If you intend making a will it is useful to have the following points decided before meeting a solicitor:

- the names and addresses of your executors, trustees and guardians (if
  applicable)

- the names and addresses of your beneficiaries and the age at which you
  would like your children (if applicable) to inherit their benefits under
  your will

- details of all your assets, including pension benefits and life policies
  that will become payable on your death. It is very important to have
  these details so that any inheritance tax implications can be examined.

After the initial meeting a draft should be sent to you for your comments.
Remember you do not have any valid will until the will has been signed
by you and by two witnesses in your presence.

After you have executed your will, the original should be kept either
by the solicitor or in a bank for safekeeping. Your solicitor will send you
a copy of your will for your records.

At any stage in the future you can amend your will, e.g. if your family
circumstances have changed or if your assets alter after the date of your
last will.

Chapter Two

Legal Issues which Arise after a Person Dies

FUNERAL ARRANGEMENTS

After a relative dies it is a very distressing time for the next of kin, whose first duty is to organise the funeral for the deceased relative. It reduces problems if the deceased has expressed his/her wishes regarding the funeral and/or cremation arrangements to the next of kin during his/her lifetime, either verbally or by a letter of wishes, which is normally retained with the will. Alternatively, it is possible for these wishes to be set out in a will but it is important to realise that these wishes are not legally binding on the next of kin or executors, even if legally expressed in a will. Yet, in the vast majority of cases, the wishes, if known beforehand, are followed out to the letter by the next of kin and/or executors. If there is any disagreement regarding the arrangements of the funeral between the next of kin and the executors, the executors are the persons legally entitled to make the final decision. Before any funeral arrangements are finalised, it is important for the executors and/or the family to ascertain from the deceased's solicitor whether any wishes have been expressed by the deceased regarding these matters. In some cases, the deceased may also have expressed a wish that their remains are to be left for medical research purposes, and again, these wishes should be ascertained before the funeral arrangements are made.

Who Are Personal Representatives?

Personal representatives are of two kinds. If appointed by a will, they are called executors. Otherwise they are known as administrators. Executors can carry out their duties immediately after someone dies. However, where administrators are acting, the ownership of the deceased's assets does not pass to the administrators until officially appointed by the court, i.e. until a grant of representation is given to them by the Probate Office in Dublin or a District Probate Registry (outside Dublin), which is proof of their status. The main difference, therefore, is that executors can sell an asset immediately after someone dies, but administrators cannot sell an asset until the grant of representation is issued a number of months later.

Executors

The first step of the executors, who are normally next of kin, is to obtain a copy of the deceased's will, usually from the deceased's solicitor, in order to verify their appointment as executors and to ascertain the wishes of the deceased as expressed in the will. Sometimes, a letter of wishes may also have been signed by the deceased. This may be with the will and may set out certain guidelines for the executors regarding the administration of the estate, which they would need to be aware of.

On receiving the copy of the will, all the executors normally meet in the office of the solicitor, who is instructed to assist them in the administration of the estate. The solicitor concerned should then explain the duties of executors.

Functions of Executors

The functions of the executors are to extract a grant of probate to the estate (i.e. all savings and property) and to administer the estate of the deceased. The powers and duties of the executors commence from the death of the deceased. From that date, the whole estate devolves or passes to the executors and they can make decisions immediately relating to the administration of the estate.

Executors Not Obliged to Act

The executors are not legally obliged to act as executors. It is only necessary for one of the executors appointed to act as executor. In addition, any executor resident outside Ireland can either act as executor personally or may execute a power of attorney and appoint someone resident in Ireland to act on their behalf. An executor may renounce the executorship, but once a person decides to take on the role of executor, he/she cannot then renounce it at a later stage. Executors may also reserve their right to act as executors, i.e. they do not act as executors initially but may apply to become executors at a later stage if the need arises.

Executors Cannot Delegate their Duties

The executors cannot delegate their authority but they can, where appropriate, appoint other persons who are experts in their fields to help them in the administration of the estate. For instance, they may employ an auctioneer to value and/or sell a property. The general rule is that executors sufficiently discharge their duty if they take all the precautions that an ordinary prudent person would take in managing similar affairs of their own.

Fees and Expenses

An executor is not entitled to receive any fees unless the executor is a professional person and the will specifies that any professional person can receive fees for acting as executor. Usually, an executor is only entitled to be reimbursed for expenses incurred during the administration period.

Ascertain Directions under the Will

The executors must determine whether there are any particular problems in following the wishes contained in the will. For instance, it is fairly common for a deceased person to leave a specific bank account to a specific beneficiary in the will. However, if this bank account is closed before the deceased dies then the legal principle of ademption operates, i.e. the beneficiary receives nothing under the will because the source of the bequest is no longer in existence.

Alternatively, there could be a problem with the execution of the will, particularly if the will was made without professional advice. For example, if the deceased signed a home-made will, the will could be defective, directions in the will might be ambiguous, the will might not dispose of all the assets or the will might not be executed correctly. In these situations an affidavit might be required from one of the witnesses to the will explaining how the will was executed. In the case of more serious problems, the court might have to determine the legal problem arising from the home-made will. If the deceased died with a mental disability, e.g. Alzheimer's disease, it is necessary for the executors to obtain an affidavit from a doctor who knew the deceased, confirming that the deceased had the necessary mental capacity to make the will at the time it was executed.

Duty to Protect Assets

The executor is also under a duty to protect the assets in the estate. For instance, the executor must ensure that all assets which need to be insured are insured for the proper market value or reinstatement value. Nevertheless, an executor is under no duty whatsoever to seek to appreciate the value of the assets during the course of the administration, but must try and protect them from perishing. If a premises is vacant, the executor should notify the insurance company, which may have certain additional requirements. It is very unusual for an insurance company to insure contents in a vacant house and it may be necessary for the executors to remove certain small valuable contents to a place of safe keeping, e.g. a bank.

Duty to Act Expeditiously

The executors have a duty to act expeditiously in the administration of the estate and it is thus imperative that the executors instruct a solicitor to administer the estate as soon as possible, or take steps themselves to obtain all the necessary information in order to obtain a grant of probate as quickly as possible after the death of the deceased. It is important to realise that if a legacy under a will is not paid within a year of the deceased's death, then the legatees are entitled to interest, presently running at 8 per cent, in addition to their legacy.

Opening an Executor's Account

All monies the executor or executors receive and all payments which they make during the administration of the estate should be transacted through an executor's bank account. Accordingly, the executor or executors should, as soon as possible, open an executor's bank account in their name(s) as executor(s) of the deceased. This, they can operate to make lodgements or to make payments. Generally, the bank account will be opened in one of the banks where the deceased had an account, but it can be opened at any bank.

TRUSTEES

Sometimes the executors may also be appointed trustees in the will, or other persons may be appointed trustees. Trustees are normally appointed in the following situations:

Where there are beneficiaries under eighteen years of age: beneficiaries under eighteen cannot inherit a bequest of money or property in their own right and their legacy or bequest must be held by trustees until they attain the age of eighteen years.

With problem beneficiaries: there may be a beneficiary who has a drink problem, a gambling problem, has a mental disability or is merely irresponsible when it comes to managing money. In this situation, a trust is normally set up for the beneficiary's lifetime and the trustees may have a discretion as to when they should make any payments for the benefit of the beneficiary concerned, depending on the terms of the trust.

With a family business/farm: if there is a family business or farm and the potential beneficiaries are still very young, the deceased may direct in the will that the trustees are to hold the business or farm on trust for a fixed number of years and then transfer the business or the farm to the beneficiaries, who in the opinion of the trustees, are the most appropriate persons to receive the bequest.

(Note: the trustees are not involved in the administration of the estate until the grant of probate is issued and the executors transfer the trust assets to the trustees.)

PROCEDURE TO TAKE OUT A GRANT OF PROBATE

Until a grant of probate issues from the Probate Office, all the assets of the deceased are usually frozen, i.e. monies in any bank accounts cannot be utilised until the grant of probate issues. The grant of probate is a document that issues from the Probate Office in the High Court Dublin or District Probate Registry and confirms:

1. That the will is a valid will.

2. That the executors who have applied for probate can now administer the estate.

3. The amount of the gross and net Irish estate.

In order to obtain a grant of probate, a number of documents must be executed by the executor(s):

An Inland Revenue Affidavit

This is a document which sets out all the assets and liabilities of the deceased at the date of death that are located in Ireland or abroad. There are frequently delays for a number of months in obtaining all this information. In addition, before the Inland Revenue affidavit is prepared, it is necessary to write to each beneficiary named in the will for details of all gifts or inheritances received from any person within the same group of relations as the deceased, including the deceased, from 2 December 1988. This information is required for the Revenue Commissioners and obtaining it from all the beneficiaries can delay the completion of the probate papers. The income tax number (RSI number) of the beneficiary will be required if the beneficiary has to pay inheritance tax or submit an inheritance tax return to the Revenue Commissioners. The Inland Revenue affidavit is sworn by the executors before an independent solicitor and is sent to the Revenue Commissioners in Dublin Castle for their attention. It is necessary to include documentary evidence in the Inland Revenue affidavit stating the assets of the deceased as at the date of death, e.g. letters from financial institutions confirming the balances in the deceased's bank accounts or building society accounts at the date of death, valuations of stocks and shares and valuations of any property and contents if required.

The Inland Revenue affidavit must be sent to the Revenue Commissioners with any probate tax which is payable. A probate tax of 2 per cent must be paid on the value of all property exceeding £40,000 in value for deaths after 1 December 1999 — other than joint property or monies paid under a superannuation scheme, e.g. a lump sum under a pension policy or anything inherited by a surviving spouse. Normally, the banks where the deceased had accounts will release the necessary funds to pay the probate tax before the grant of probate has been issued. When the Revenue Commissioners receive the correct amount of probate tax payable, they will certify the amount of the gross assets and the net assets on the back of the Inland Revenue affidavit and return it within a few weeks of receiving it.

An Oath of Executor

This document is an oath sworn by the executor(s), whereby they undertake to pay all the debts and liabilities of the deceased and discharge all the bequests and legacies contained in the will.

The certified Inland Revenue affidavit and the oath of executor(s), together with the original will, are lodged in the Probate Office in the Four Courts or District Probate Registry along with other miscellaneous documents and the required fee. The grant of probate normally issues within a few weeks after the date that the papers are lodged.

PROCEDURE TO TAKE OUT LETTERS OF ADMINISTRATION INTESTATE

Where there is property or assets in the deceased's name and the deceased dies without a will, i.e. intestate, the surviving spouse, if any, or any one or more of the next of kin must apply to the Probate Office for a grant of administration (called Letters of Administration Intestate) before the deceased's estate can be administered.

If a deceased dies without a will, his/her estate is distributed in the following manner:

- where there is a surviving spouse but no children, the entire estate is distributed to the surviving spouse

- where there is a surviving spouse and children, the surviving spouse is entitled to inherit two-thirds of the estate and the remaining one-third is distributed among the surviving children of the deceased

- where there is no surviving spouse or children, the deceased's estate is inherited by his/her surviving parent(s)

- where there is no surviving spouse, children or parent, then the estate is divided among the deceased's surviving brothers or sisters. If any brother or sister has predeceased the deceased, then the share of that brother or sister is inherited by the children of that deceased brother or sister, i.e. the nephews and nieces of the deceased.

In order to obtain Letters of Administration Intestate, the following documents must be executed by the administrators, who are one or more of the next of kin who inherit a share of the deceased's estate:

- an Inland Revenue affidavit

- an oath of administrator — this document is an oath under which the administrators swear to undertake to pay all the debts and liabilities of the deceased and distribute the estate among the appropriate next of kin. It is more or less the same document as an oath of executor, except that it is called an oath of administrator

- an administration bond — this is a special document required by the Probate Office when the deceased dies intestate. The bond must be executed by the applicant, usually with an insurance company which guarantees to pay up to double the gross assets of the estate in the event of the estate being dissipated by the administrator.

Where an insurance company is joining in the bond, then a premium must be paid for the bond. The premium is based on the amount of the gross assets of the estate. On assets up to £75,000, the premium is approximately £75. On assets exceeding £75,000, the premium is approximately £1 for every £1,000 of assets. There is also a tax of 2 per cent payable on the premium.

It is possible to avoid the expense of an insurance company if one or two individuals are prepared to act as guarantors. In this situation, one person must swear that their own personal assets are worth more than double the gross assets of the deceased's estate. Alternatively, two people can swear that each of them have personal assets that are equal to all the gross assets in the deceased's estate. The affidavit verifying an individual's gross assets is called a "Justification of Surety".

The Inland Revenue affidavit, together with the oath of administrator, the administration bond and other miscellaneous documents as well as the appropriate fee, are lodged in the Probate Office in the Four Courts or District Probate Registry in order to obtain the letters of administration intestate, which is the equivalent of a grant of probate when there is no will.

AFTER THE GRANT OF PROBATE ISSUES

The original grant of probate and certified copies of same are sent to all the financial institutions so that the monies in such institutions can be lodged into the executor's bank account. If there are any stocks and shares, a copy of the grant is sent to the registrars of the various companies so that the share certificates can be noted in the names of the executors. In due course, the executor(s) can sell the stocks and shares or transfer them into the names of the beneficiaries.

Income Tax

The income tax affairs of the deceased must be finalised up to the date of death. This is normally done by the deceased's professional advisors or by the executors themselves in straightforward cases. There may also be additional tax liabilities after the date of death and the executors are personally liable for such taxes if they distribute the assets of the estate before paying these taxes.

Capital Gains Tax

It may be necessary to submit capital gains tax returns up to the date of death with the income tax returns. Furthermore, if any assets are sold after the date of death by the executors, e.g. shares or property, then there could be capital gains tax payable, which the executors will have to discharge before completing the administration of the estate. In this situation, capital gains tax is paid on the difference between the date of death value and the amount the asset is sold for.

Irish Inheritance Tax

If any beneficiary is liable to Irish inheritance tax on receipt of his/her legacy or bequest under the deceased's will, then such tax must be paid within four months of receiving the benefit. For practical purposes, the Revenue Commissioners normally treat the date of the grant of probate as the date on which the beneficiary is deemed to receive the inheritance. Accordingly, the beneficiary must pay any inheritance tax due within four months of the issue of the grant of probate. If the tax is not paid within the time required, then interest on the outstanding tax is payable at the rate of 12 per cent per annum.

It is extremely important for the executor(s) to make sure that all the beneficiaries pay their correct amount of inheritance tax on the benefit they receive under the will. If the beneficiaries do not pay the inheritance tax due, then the Revenue Commissioners are legally entitled to claim the tax from the executor(s).

If any inheritance tax is payable, then an inheritance tax return must be completed by the beneficiary and sent to the Revenue Commissioners with the appropriate tax required. Usually, the solicitor acting for the executor(s) will prepare the inheritance tax returns for the beneficiaries.

RIGHTS OF A SURVIVING SPOUSE

Under the Succession Act 1965, a surviving spouse is legally entitled to a specific share of the estate of a deceased spouse depending on whether the deceased had any children. This right, called a "legal right share", arises where there is a will and the surviving spouse has never waived his/her rights and is entitled to make a claim. If the deceased had children, the surviving spouse is entitled to a one-third share of the estate. If there are no children, the spouse is entitled to a one-half share of the estate. The executors are obliged to notify a surviving spouse of this right of election after the grant of probate has been issued. The Succession Act 1965 provides that the surviving spouse must exercise his/her right of election within six months of receiving such notification from the executors or within one year of the issue of the grant of probate, whichever is the later. It is important to remember that a surviving spouse will generally automatically inherit any property held jointly with his/her deceased spouse by survivorship. This joint property is not taken into account in calculating the legal right share of the surviving spouse who can claim a legal right share in the remainder of the estate owned by the deceased.

CHARITABLE BEQUESTS

If the will provides for bequests or legacies to a specific charity or charities, then there is a set procedure which must be followed. Under the Charities Act legislation, the Charitable Commissioners who administer charities must be informed of all charitable bequests to charities under wills. After the death of the deceased, the charities will normally be informed of the terms of the bequest and the executors are then obliged to obtain from them a letter of awareness, i.e. a letter from them stating that they have been informed of the bequest. All the letters of awareness from the various charitable beneficiaries should then be sent to the Charity Commissioners.

OBLIGATIONS UNDER SOCIAL WELFARE LEGISLATION

If the deceased was in receipt of an Old Age Non-Contributory Pension or another non-contributory social welfare payment, then the executors are under a statutory duty to forward a copy of the Inland Revenue affidavit to the Department of Social Welfare not less than three months before commencing to distribute the assets of the deceased. The department must reply within three months if any monies should be paid from the estate to the Department of Social Welfare. The estate can be distributed without making any payments to the Department of Social Welfare if no request for payment is made within the three month period.

The background to this legislation is that most non-contributory social welfare payments, including Old Age Non-Contributory pensions, are subject to a means test. If the deceased was receiving the social welfare payments but was not legally entitled to receive these payments or the full extent of these payments because of additional means which the deceased had during his/her lifetime, then the Department of Social Welfare looks for a refund of the social welfare payments that should not have been paid during the deceased's lifetime. In certain cases, many thousands of pounds may have to be refunded to the Department of Social Welfare. Thus, it is imperative that the executors ascertain, as soon as possible, whether any such refunds have to be made from the estate to the department. Any executors who distribute assets of a deceased person without paying any sum due to the Department of Social Welfare, can be made personally liable to repay the appropriate amounts to the department.

JOINT BANK ACCOUNTS

It often happens that an older person opens a joint bank account with a relative or friend to enable that person to have access to his/her funds. This can cause problems, however, should the other person die, as the question of who is entitled to the beneficial ownership of the monies in the account then arises.

Where the deceased opened a joint bank account with someone other than a spouse or child, it is imperative for the executor(s) to ascertain who is legally entitled to inherit the monies in the joint bank account on the deceased's death, and the executors may have to obtain legal advice on this matter. Obviously, if the deceased has expressed any wishes regarding the monies in this joint bank account, then it would be important for the executors to ascertain these wishes as soon as possible and to obtain the necessary legal advice concerning the ownership of the monies in the joint account before any distribution is made.

If the survivor in a joint bank account is not a surviving spouse but is some other relative or friend, the funds in the account, if over £5,000 and on deposit, cannot be released to the survivor without a letter of clearance from the Revenue Commissioners.

With regard to a joint bank account in the names of both husband and wife, a surviving spouse is not required to present a tax clearance certificate and the funds, no matter how large, can be released automatically (see Chapter One for more information).

ASSETS OUTSIDE IRELAND

Quite often the deceased may have a bank account outside Ireland, e.g. in Northern Ireland or in England. Alternatively, the deceased may have English shares. In these situations, it will normally be necessary, unless the value of the assets is small, to take out a grant of probate in the country where the assets are located. It will usually be necessary to instruct solicitors in the foreign country to assist in taking out the grant of probate in that jurisdiction. The assets in the foreign country cannot be realised until the foreign grant is taken out, which may delay the administration of the estate. The foreign grant cannot be applied for until after the Irish grant of probate has issued, if the deceased died domiciled in Ireland.

LEGAL RIGHTS OF CHILDREN

It is very important that executors are aware or informed of the legal rights of children under their parent's will. A child, unlike a spouse, is not entitled to a specified share in a deceased parent's estate as a right. However, any child who feels aggrieved with a legacy, bequest or share which he/she may have received under a parent's will may make an application to court asking the court to find that the parent has failed in his/her moral duty to make a proper provision for that child in accordance with his/her means, whether by will or otherwise. Each case is decided on its own merit and the court looks at the situation from the point of view of a "prudent and just" parent. The legal right share of a surviving spouse or bequest to a spouse cannot be set aside in order to give a child a share.

Obviously, if the executors are aware of such a possible claim, they cannot make any distribution from the estate. A claim by a child to a greater share of a parent's estate cannot be made more than six months after the grant of probate issues.

STATUTORY NOTICE TO CREDITORS

Where the deceased died owning a business, it is important for the executors to publish a statutory notice to creditors. Under the Succession Act 1965, the executors can publish a notice in a newspaper advertising claims from creditors. If such claims are not made before the date specified, then the executors are absolutely protected against any subsequent claims by a creditor and can distribute the estate without any legal claim after the expiry of the relevant date.

FINALISING THE ADMINISTRATION OF THE ESTATE

Before the estate is completely wound up, the executors must obtain:

- receipts from all the beneficiaries in respect of the benefits they received under the will

- certificates of discharge from the Revenue Commissioners for any inheritance tax payable by the beneficiaries

- receipts from the Collector General for all outstanding liabilities to capital gains tax and income tax

- a cash statement showing how the assets were distributed during the administration of the estate and how all the debts and liabilities were discharged.

LEGAL FEES

Solicitors generally follow a guideline regarding the nature of the fees that may be charged in the administration of estates. Using this guideline, the level of fees is based on the value of an estate as follows:

- 3.5 per cent on the value of gross assets up to the amount of £10,000

- 3 per cent on the next £10,000

- 2.5 per cent on the balance of the gross assets

- in addition, there would be VAT at 21 per cent as well as outlay.

Most solicitors would normally charge fees using this guideline. Alternatively, legal fees may be based on the time involved in administering an estate. Sometimes, because of unforeseen complications or difficulties, the time involved in administering the estate exceeds the scale fee and the fee might then be charged on a time basis. On the other hand, the scale fee might also be reduced by solicitors where the administration might be straightforward and might not involve a substantial amount of time. Under the Solicitors' Acts, the solicitor is obliged to agree on the basis of charging the legal fees before the administration commences.

It should also be pointed out that the Probate Office will assist executors who wish to personally take out a grant of probate without instructing a solicitor. However, after the grant of probate issues, executors may have to consult a solicitor to prepare the necessary documentation if a house or other property has to be transferred to one or more beneficiaries. In addition, there may be complicated tax returns which might have to be made after the grant of probate issues and it may be possible for beneficiaries to reduce inheritance tax by taking legal advice from a solicitor or other professional advisor.

Chapter Three

Legal Arrangements for Managing Financial Affairs when an Older Person Becomes Unwell

JOINT BANK ACCOUNTS

It often happens that an older person opens a joint account with a relative or friend to enable that person to have access to his/her funds. It is a particularly useful means of dealing with one's financial affairs when an older person has mobility problems, is ill or is unable to take responsibility for maintaining an account on his/her own.

Opening the Account

Any person can open a bank account when that person has the necessary mental capacity. A bank or building society will not open an account if they believe the person opening the account is being coerced or unduly influenced by someone else. When an account is opened an account holder may authorise the bank to accept cheques if signed by another individual. There is a standard form that is signed by an account holder which gives a sample of the signature of the person being authorised.

Operating the Account

If it appears that an account holder does not understand the transactions involved in operating a bank account due to mental incapacity the account will be frozen. In this situation, the account can only be utilised if an enduring power of attorney is registered on behalf of the account holder or if the account holder is made a ward of court. However, if the only payments from an account are to a nursing home, the bank may be willing to give the benefit of any doubt as to the mental capacity of the account holder and continue to allow the payments.

If a joint account is opened, the bank can be authorised to honour cheques signed by both account holders or by only one. In the case of a joint account, the bank has a contractual duty to each account holder. If one account holder is mentally incapacitated, the legal authority to operate the account is revoked and the account cannot be used by the other joint account holder.

The production of a consistent signature is normal when operating a bank account. If the physical ability to sign becomes impaired, arrangements should be made for some form of mark to be accepted or for someone else to sign. The bank may require medical evidence of capacity in this situation. Direct debits or standing orders will also be cancelled if the account holder becomes mentally incapacitated.

Death of One Account Holder

If one of the persons holding a joint account dies, the question arises as to who is entitled to the beneficial ownership of the monies in the joint account. Definite legal considerations apply when determining this matter, depending on:

- the intention of the parties
- the extent or otherwise to which they contributed to the account
- the terms of their contract with the bank, e.g. where the bank is instructed that the money should be paid to the surviving joint account holder on the death of either party.

Recommendation

It is most advisable that if a person, particularly an older person, considers opening a joint bank account, they should leave written instructions with the bank and with their family as to who is to inherit the money on their death. Their intentions should also be made clear to the second person named in the account, and if possible referred to in their will (see Chapter One for more information).

AGENCY ARRANGEMENTS FOR SOCIAL WELFARE PAYMENTS

The Department of Social, Community and Family Affairs has the power under social welfare legislation to make payments to a third party acting on behalf of the recipient. The person to whom a social welfare benefit is payable may nominate another person to receive that benefit on his/her behalf.

An agent appointed under social welfare legislation may deal only with social welfare payments; he or she has no power to deal with other financial matters.

In practice, the Department of Social, Community and Family Affairs recognises different types of agents:

"Type 1"Agent

A "Type 1" agent can be appointed on a temporary or permanent basis. Under this type of agency, the money is payable to a person entitled and all correspondence relating to it is addressed to that person. Nevertheless, an agent is empowered to collect the money on behalf of the recipient and is under a legal duty to give it to the recipient.

Temporary Agency

A temporary "Type 1" agency can be created where the social welfare claimant signs the back page of each voucher. Payment by means of a temporary "Type 1" agency by the post office official is discretionary. The voucher must be signed on each occasion by both the recipient and the agent. The written authority created by the act of signing the form only entitles the agent to actually collect the money and hand it over to the person entitled to it.

Permanent Agency

The Department of Social, Community and Family Affairs may make payments to a person nominated by the recipient. If a recipient is unable to act, the Minister may appoint some other person to exercise rights on behalf of the person entitled under social welfare legislation.

"Type 2" Agency

A "Type 2" agency arises where a social welfare officer decides (usually as a result of representations from family members and medical practitioners) that an individual is incapable of acting and that an agent should be appointed. A social welfare officer will usually call to visit the legally entitled recipient to assess the circumstances and the needs of that individual. The agent nominated is often a family member or the matron of a nursing home or hospital. A "Type 2" agency often arises in the context of mental incapacity and all correspondence in respect of the social welfare payments will be directed to the appointed agent.

POWERS OF ATTORNEY

What Is a Power of Attorney?

A power of attorney is a legal arrangement whereby one person (the donor) gives authority to another or others (the attorney/attorneys) to act on his/her behalf. The attorney under a power of attorney is required to act as if he/she were the donor. Decisions should be based, if possible, on the wishes expressed by the donor prior to becoming less able to deal with his/her affairs. The power can be general or limited. If it is general, the attorney can do anything that the donor could have lawfully done. However, if the power of attorney is limited, the attorney may have the authority to deal with only one matter, e.g. the sale of a house. The power could also stipulate that it is only to remain in force for a specified time, e.g. one year. The donor can still act on his/her own behalf after granting a power of attorney.

When Are they Necessary?

Powers of attorney are frequently used when a person is going abroad, either for a long or short period of time, and that person has some legal transaction to complete here in Ireland while abroad. For example, the owners of a house might have to move abroad before their house in Ireland is sold and someone here in Ireland has to sell the house on their behalf after they have left.

Elderly people can also use powers of attorney to enable their business affairs to be dealt with by someone else. They are commonly used by elderly people who are confined to a house or nursing home and where, for instance, they are not mobile enough to visit their bank. In such situations, adult children or other relatives can be authorised, under the power of attorney, to operate bank and building society accounts and deal with investments on behalf of their relatives.

The Form and Operation of the Power of Attorney

The power of attorney consists of a legal document showing that the attorney has the power to act on the donor's behalf. It must be in writing and signed in the presence of a witness. A precedent form of power of attorney is set out in the Powers of Attorney Act 1996. However, legal advice should be obtained whenever a power of attorney is needed. The original power of attorney, or a copy certified by the donor or a solicitor to be true copies of the original, can be produced to banks, building societies, insurance companies, etc. as sufficient legal authority for the attorney to act on behalf of the donor in relation to the donor's affairs.

Appointing Attorneys

One or more people can be appointed attorneys by the donor. If two or more people are appointed, the document should state whether the attorneys are to act jointly or severally, i.e. the attorneys may either act together or independently of each other. If appointed jointly, all the attorneys must make decisions jointly and one joint attorney cannot act on his/her own without the authority of the other attorneys. If one joint attorney dies or becomes mentally incapacitated or disqualified, the remaining attorneys may continue to act unless the power of attorney specifies otherwise. If two or more persons are appointed attorneys to act jointly and severally, then all the attorneys do not have to make decisions jointly and one attorney can act independently of the others, which the others are legally bound by. Joint and several attorneys should be appointed if one attorney goes abroad frequently or if one of the attorneys is elderly.

Who Should Be an Attorney?

The attorney can be a relative, friend, professional person or even a bank. The attorney should be a person whom the donor can trust and rely on. Sometimes the donor might prefer that his/her relatives or friends are not involved in his/her financial affairs and might prefer to appoint a professional advisor. Usually, however, a professional person will charge fees for acting as attorney.

Duties of Attorneys

If the attorney is a relative or a friend of the donor, there is generally no obligation on that person to act as attorney. Nevertheless, if the attorney is a professional person and is getting paid for acting as attorney, there may be a legal obligation on that attorney to act under the power of attorney. The attorney, if acting, must follow the terms of the power of attorney.

The attorney is obliged to act in good faith in all his/her dealings as attorney — he/she must not put himself in a position where his duty to the donor conflicts with a duty to someone else.

The attorney is obliged to keep accurate accounts and records. An attorney must use such skill as he/she possesses and show such care and skill as he/she normally would in conducting his/her own affairs. If the attorney is being paid, he/she must exercise the care, skill and diligence of a reasonable person or with proper professional competence if he/she is a professional person.

An attorney is not entitled to make a profit from acting as attorney without the consent of the donor.

The attorney cannot appoint someone else to act as attorney and must act personally in the performance of his/her duties. However, having decided on a course of action, an attorney has the authority to employ, if necessary, solicitors, estate agents, accountants, builders and so on to implement that decision.

An attorney is under a duty to keep the donor's affairs confidential, unless the donor authorises the attorney to disclose them.

Termination of Power of Attorney

The donor can cancel or revoke the powers of attorney at any time. It is advisable to do this in writing and inform the attorney and all financial institutions acting on the power of attorney.

If the power of attorney is for a stated period of time, it expires when that period comes to an end. Similarly, if the power is granted to authorise a single act, such as selling a house, it expires when the act is completed.

If the donor develops a mental illness, such as senile dementia or Alzheimer's disease, the power of attorney is no longer exercisable by the attorney. It was to obviate this defect that enduring powers of attorney were legalised under the Powers of Attorney Act 1996, which came into operation on 1 August 1996.

ENDURING POWERS OF ATTORNEY

What Is an Enduring Power of Attorney?

An enduring power of attorney (EPA) is a power of attorney which can only operate if the donor (the person who creates the document) becomes mentally incapable of managing his/her affairs. As long as the donor is well, the enduring power of attorney cannot be acted on by the attorney.

Why an Enduring Power of Attorney May Be Necessary

In 1995 in Ireland, there were approximately 400,000 people aged over 65, i.e. 11 per cent of the population. In 1991 there were 78,800 persons aged 80 or over. It is estimated that 5 per cent of people over 65 suffer from some form of senile dementia in Ireland and that there are over 25,000 suffering from Alzheimer's disease. It is therefore advisable that anyone over 65 should consider making an enduring power of attorney.

As already mentioned, an ordinary power of attorney can no longer be valid if the donor becomes mentally incapable of managing his/her affairs. In such a situation the donor would have to be made a ward of court where the financial affairs would be managed under the supervision of the wards of court office and the High Court, where appropriate. Wardship applications can be a stressful and expensive process, which can be avoided by making an enduring power of attorney. It is for this additional reason, that legislation was introduced providing for enduring powers of attorney.

The Form of Enduring Power of Attorney

The form of an enduring power of attorney must be in the form as set out in the Ministerial Regulations applying to the Powers of Attorney Act 1996. The form is very different from the format of an ordinary power of attorney and if the correct format is not used, the EPA is defective and invalid.

Attorney Powers under the Powers of Attorney Act 1996

The Powers of Attorney Act 1996 provides that an EPA may give the attorney power to act on the donor's behalf in relation to any one or more of the following:

- all or a specified part of the donor's property
- all or a specified part of the donor's business or financial affairs
- to do other specified things
- to make personal care decisions affecting the donor
- to make appropriate gifts to any of the donor's relations or friends or favourite charity of the donor
- to make any such powers subject to conditions and restrictions.

Personal Care Decisions

The power to give the attorney the right to make personal care decisions affecting the donor is a welcome additional power which was only inserted in the draft legislation at a late stage and after much lobbying. However, the donor is under no legal obligation to give the attorney power to make any personal care decisions and can limit the attorney's role to their business or financial affairs only. The attorney can also restrict the number of personal care decisions the donor can make.

Personal care decisions must be made in the donor's best interest and include making the following decisions:

- where the donor should live

- with whom the donor should live

- who the donor should see and not see

- what training or rehabilitation the donor should receive

- the donor's diet and dress

- who may inspect the donor's personal papers

- what housing, social welfare or other benefits the donor needs.

Where practical and appropriate, the attorney should consult with members of the donor's family or other interested persons regarding personal care decisions. The donor can also name a person or persons whom the donor should consult before making any personal care decisions.

A Note of Caution

An enduring power of attorney is potentially extremely flexible and the power to impose restrictions and conditions may be very valuable. Nevertheless, the fact remains that the less authority that is given to the attorney by the donor in the enduring power of attorney, the greater the risk that the attorney would be unable to manage all the property and affairs of the donor. In this situation, it is possible that the donor may have to be made a ward of court because of unduly restrictive conditions contained in the enduring power of attorney.

Regulations

Regulations under the 1996 Act provide for the following in relation to an enduring power of attorney:

1. The specific format of an EPA.

2. (a) The various options which the donor has when granting an EPA.
    (b) A statement signed by the donor that he/she has read the explana-

tory information regarding the creation of an EPA or has had it read to him/her.

3. (a) The duties and obligations which an attorney may have under EPA.
   (b) A statement signed by the attorney that he/she understands these duties and obligations.

4. The obligation on the attorney to keep adequate accounts.

5. The remuneration, if any, of the attorney who is entitled to out-of-pocket expenses, even if no form of remuneration is provided for in the EPA.

6. The execution requirements of an EPA.

7. A statement by a solicitor in the format provided that he/she is satisfied the donor understood the effect of the EPA.

8. A statement by a medical practitioner in the format provided, that, in his opinion, the donor had the mental capacity at the time of execution to understand the effect of creating an EPA.

Who May Be Attorney?

The Act provides that an attorney under an EPA must:

• be over eighteen or be a trust corporation (as defined)

• not have been adjudicated bankrupt

• not have been convicted of an offence involving fraud or dishonesty or an offence against the personal property of the donor

• not be the owner of a nursing home or be employed by the nursing home where the donor resides.

An EPA in favour of a spouse shall cease to be in force if there is a subsequent legal separation between the spouses or certain other matrimonial proceedings between them.

A donor may also appoint more than one person to be an attorney and may specify that the attorneys are appointed to act either jointly, or jointly and severally.

Signing of an Enduring Power of Attorney

The donor must sign the EPA in the presence of a solicitor, who must then sign a certificate in the format, provided that he/she is satisfied that the donor understood the document. Sometimes the donor may be in the early stages of Alzheimer's disease but has lucid intervals. It might be important to have the document signed in the presence of both the solicitor and the doctor in these circumstances. The doctor can then certify that the donor had the necessary mental capacity to understand the document when it was signed. The attorney(s) must sign the document after the donor in the presence of a witness, who can also be the same solicitor. In signing the EPA, the attorney confirms that he/she understands the obligations it imposes. The attorney also acknowledges the duty to register the EPA if the donor's mental health deteriorates to such an extent that the donor is or is becoming, mentally incapable of managing his/her affairs.

However, the attorney can withdraw his/her consent to act as attorney at any time before the EPA is registered. After the EPA is registered, the attorney can only be relieved of his/her duties as attorney with the consent of the court.

Notice of Execution of an EPA

Under the regulations, the donor is obliged to notify at least two people (who are not the attorneys) regarding the execution of the EPA. At least one of them is required by the regulations to be:

• the donor's spouse, if living with the donor

• a child of the donor, if the former does not apply

• a relative of the donor, if neither of the above apply. A relative is defined as a parent, brother, sister, grandchild, widow or widower of a child of the donor or a nephew or niece.

The other notice party can be a non-relative. An attorney cannot be one of the notice parties. If, for instance, the spouse and only son are the attorneys, then notice must be given to two others, of whom one must be a relative of the donor. The prescribed form of notice is contained in the Third Schedule of the Regulations. If there are no such relatives, the donor can nominate other parties. Whoever is nominated to receive the notice of execution of the enduring power of attorney by the donor will be entitled to receive notice of the application to register the enduring power of attorney when that time comes, unless they have died, become mentally incapable themselves, or it is not possible to locate them.

Application of Registration

An enduring power of attorney cannot be acted on until registered. In practice, it would only be registered in a minority of cases. Section 9(I) of the Act states as follows:

> If an attorney under an enduring power of attorney has reason to believe that the donor is or is becoming mentally incapable, the attorney shall, as soon as practicable, make an application to the court for registration of the instrument creating the power.

Under section 4 of the Act, mental incapacity in relation to an individual means incapacity by reason of a mental condition to manage and administer his/her own property and affairs. In summary, before the attorney has a duty to register the enduring power of attorney, it is necessary to prove two things:

1.   That the donor is suffering from a mental disorder.

2.   That because of the mental disorder and mental incapacity, the person is incapable of managing and administering his/her property and affairs.

These two conditions do not automatically coincide. People suffering from a mental disorder might be quite capable of looking after their financial affairs and those who are not mentally disordered may be completely hopeless in running their affairs — they could be disorganised, uninterested, foolish, prodigal or just lazy.

A medical certificate from a doctor is required to prove that the donor is or is becoming incapable of managing his/her affairs.

Form of Registration Notice

A notice (in the form provided in the Fourth Schedule of the Regulations) of the attorney's application to register the EPA must be served on the donor and also on the people who were notified of the execution of the EPA and are named in it. Any person served with this notice can object to the registration by sending the grounds for objection to the wards of court office within five weeks on receipt of the notice.

If any of the people notified at that time are dead or are themselves mentally incapable or cannot be located, then the surviving "notice party" should be notified. If none of the original notice parties are alive or cannot be located or if they have all become mentally incapable, then at least three relatives should be notified. The Act contains a list of relatives to be notified, commencing with the donor's spouse and then passing on in descending order to the donor's children, parents, brothers or sisters. The full list is set out in Article 3 of Part 1 of the First Schedule to the Act.

Once the attorney has applied for registration, he/she may act on the EPA, namely to take action under the power to maintain the donor and prevent loss to the donor's property or savings. He/she may also make any personal care decisions that are authorised and cannot be deferred until the registration has been completed.

ADDITIONAL DUTIES OF AN ATTORNEY UNDER AN EPA

As well as making decisions regarding the business and financial affairs of the donor and personal care decisions (if permitted), the attorney has the following powers:

Needs

The attorney may use the donor's assets, savings or monies to provide for the attorney's needs or the needs of any other persons, e.g. a spouse and children, if the donor would normally have provided for these needs. "Needs" is not defined but probably includes food, housing, clothing, education, holidays, etc. The amount to be spent on the needs for someone else other than the donor depends on what the donor would have done.

The question for the attorney to ask in all cases is: "What, on the assumption that the donor had full capacity, would he have spent on meeting the particular needs concerned?"

Gifts

The attorney may also make gifts if the EPA permits it. The gifts allowed by the legislation are normally gifts at Christmas, Easter, birthdays, weddings or gifts to a charity. An individual who receives gifts must be related to or connected with the donor. The value of any gift must not be unreasonable, taking into account, in particular, the extent of the donor's assets.

Keeping of Accounts

Under the legislation, an attorney is obliged to keep adequate accounts relating to the management of the property and affairs of the donor, and especially any expenditure incurred on behalf of the donor. The legislation does not specify what is meant by adequate accounts but, at a minimum, bank statements should be kept which record all financial transactions.

Advantages of an Enduring Power of Attorney

The advantages of an EPA are that the donor is able to choose the person who will deal with his/her personal affairs and/or make personal care decisions affecting him/her. It is relatively cheap and easy to set up and can be done with little formality. It is easy to operate, involves no annual fees and there is no need to produce annual accounts on a regular basis. The attorney is expected to use his discretion but there is a procedure whereby another person may challenge the conduct of the attorney.

Disadvantages of an Enduring Power of Attorney

The procedure can only be available if the donor has sufficient mental capacity to understand the nature of the document, and it ceases to operate if the attorney dies or becomes incapable (unless there are two attorneys appointed or a substitute attorney appointed). However, there is no effective supervision or obligation on the attorney to visit the donor regularly, and the attorney's authority may be challenged on each occasion that he purports to act.

In brief, an EPA is strongly recommended for anyone who wants to minimise the legal problems his/her family may face if he/she should become mentally incapacitated in the future.

WARDS OF COURT

One of the benefits of modern society is that with the improvement in healthcare, many people are living longer than in the past. Unfortunately, with the increase in the number of older people, there are more people in our society suffering from senile dementia or other illnesses that affect their mental capacity to look after their affairs. When this situation arises, an elderly person may have to be made a ward of court if no enduring power of attorney had been executed previously or if the elderly person does not have the sufficient mental capacity to make an enduring power of attorney.

A ward of court is a person who is declared to be of unsound mind and incapable of managing his/her person or property, i.e. the ward cannot look after himself/herself physically and cannot manage his/her finances and pay everyday bills.

What Does Wardship Mean?

The principle purpose of wardship is to protect the property of the ward and to manage it for the ward's benefit and the ward's dependants (if there are any). When a person has been taken into wardship, it means that the President of the High Court is satisfied on the basis of the medical evidence available to him that that person should be deemed to be of unsound mind and is incapable of managing his/her affairs.

In a small number of cases, a person can be taken into wardship primarily for the protection of his/her person. This would usually arise in the case of a person suffering from a mental handicap rather than a psychiatric illness.

How Does a Person Become a Ward of Court?

In the majority of cases, i.e. where the person's savings or property is worth more than £5,000, a solicitor is instructed either by a social worker or often by a member of the proposed ward's family that a wardship application may be necessary. The first step is to obtain two medical reports from two medical practitioners, usually on oath, reporting on the health of the proposed ward. The reports should specify the particular medical condition from which the person is suffering, e.g. brain haemorrhage, Alzheimer's disease, senile dementia, etc. and whether this is likely to be long-term. The reports should also state that the person is incapable of managing his/her affairs. The court will also appoint its own doctor to prepare a third medical report and if all the medical reports agree that the person cannot manage his/her personal affairs, then a wardship order will normally be made.

Who Can Apply to Make a Person a Ward of Court?

As mentioned, an application to bring a person to wardship is usually (but not always) made by a member of the family. The application can also be made by the proposed ward's solicitor or doctor or by the hospital authorities if the ward is a patient in a hospital. Any concerned person can notify the Registrar of wards of court of the need to bring someone into wardship, but does not necessarily have to make the actual wardship application.

The application for wardship must be sworn by the applicant and, in most cases, must be lodged in the wards of court office with two medical reports. The application must set out details of the medical condition, next of kin, assets and income of the proposed ward.

If the court is satisfied that there is sufficient medical evidence to consider making the person a ward of court, the court, i.e. the President of the High Court, will make an order (called an "Inquiry Order"). This simply means that the application for wardship should proceed further. The wards of court office will then ask one of its doctors, called a medical visitor, to examine the person and furnish a confidential report to the court. The court will then usually direct that a copy of the application should be served personally on the proposed ward, who is given seven days to object to any wardship order.

Where the proposed ward has objected to the application, an inquiry regarding his/her mental capacity may be held before a jury. Where no objection has been made, the judge will normally make an order in the following terms:

- that the person be taken under the wardship of the court

- that the ward be detained in a certain residence, nursing home or institution, usually where the ward is already residing

- that the applicant must now file a statement of facts, normally within 21 days.

The statement of facts is sworn by the applicant and sets out a number of matters, including who should be appointed committee of the ward and make suggestions as to what is to happen to the ward's property, e.g. whether the ward's house, if any, should be sold or let. It should also state the present and future cost of maintenance of the ward, e.g. the amount of the nursing home fees.

An official of the wards of court office generally meets with the applicant's solicitor to agree on the terms of the wardship order, which is then submitted to the judge for formal approval.

The judge will normally appoint a committee of the person and of the estate of the ward. The committee is normally one or more close relations or friends. However, the ward's solicitor or even the general solicitor for minors and wards of court can act as committee where necessary. This may occur for example, where there is no suitable relative who is prepared to act or where there is a disagreement among a ward's relatives about how his/her affairs should be managed. The general solicitor is a qualified solicitor in the service of the State. The term "committee" is used because the affairs of the ward are "committed" to another person or persons. The committee may consist of one person. The committee has no inherent power or authority and can only act as specifically authorised by the court.

The committee of the person is similar to a guardian and has a duty to look after the physical welfare of the ward. This committee would apply to court regarding healthcare decisions of the ward. For example, under the legislation no general anaesthetic or operation affecting the ward should take place without the approval of the President of the High Court, unless emergency treatment is required.

The committee of the estate is similar to a trustee and can make representations to the wards of court office regarding the ward's property and investments. Nevertheless, the property of the ward is not transferred into the committee's name but is invested by the wards of court office on behalf of the ward. In practice, the duties and functions of the committee of the person and the estate often overlap and merge. Consequently, it is common practice for the same person (or persons) to be appointed both committee of the person and the estate. The committee will normally be authorised to transfer all monies in any bank account or building society account, etc. to the wards of court office for reinvestment under its control. Stocks and shares may be sold or alternatively, control is given to the wards of court office. If a property is involved, the committee will be responsible for selling it or letting it and must account for the net proceeds of sale or the rental income to the wards of court office.

If there is a sale of property, the property cannot be sold for less than the reserve price placed on the property by the ward of court's valuer.

The committee is also entitled, when authorised, to receive monies and make payments, e.g. collect pensions, receive dividends, pay outgoings (maintenance fees to hospitals or nursing homes, etc.) or purchase items for the ward's benefit.

The committee must lodge all monies received on behalf of the ward to a bank account designated as a committee account. The committee must file annual accounts for all sums received and disbursed. Annual income tax returns must also be submitted by the committee on behalf of the ward to the inspector of taxes. The committee will also have to take out an insurance bond as a protection of the ward's assets if the committee is in receipt of the ward's income.

Can a Ward Resume the Management of His/Her Own Affairs?

The answer is yes. Any application by a ward to be discharged from wardship must be made to the Registrar of the wards of court in writing by the ward or his solicitor. Such an application must provide medical evidence that the ward is now of sound mind and capable of managing his/her affairs. The President of the High Court will consider this application on the basis of the medical evidence available to him.

What Happens to a Ward's Property when He/She Dies?

On the death of a ward, after the discharge of his/her debts and when a grant of probate or administration has issued, his/her estate is distributed amongst the people entitled, either in accordance with the terms of the ward's will or among his/her closest next of kin if there is no will.

It is necessary for a formal application to be made to conclude the wardship proceedings. Pending this, the funds are made available by the court to pay expenses, such as funeral expenses, nursing home charges and probate tax.

The officials in the wards of court office are extremely helpful in discussing practical problems that may arise with the ward of court. Wardship proceedings can be stressful for both the next of kin and their solicitor, and the wards of court office is particularly sensitive in handling delicate matters which arise from time to time.

TRUSTS

The use of trusts or settlement is one way of handling the financial affairs of another person, whether or not that person is incapable of dealing with his/her own affairs.

A trust exists where a person (the trustee) holds the property of another (the settlor) for the benefit of named people (the beneficiaries). The beneficiaries may be the settlor or other people.

The trust may be created by a will or a legal document which takes effect during the settlor's lifetime, normally a declaration of trust called a "settlement".

Trustees hold and manage the trust property and may be given discretion to distribute capital and income for a particular beneficiary or beneficiaries. The trustees are normally given powers to purchase assets and services for the use or benefit of the beneficiaries rather than handing over the money. There is no supervision of the conduct of the trustees, as long as they carry out the terms of the trust. If they are given a wide discretion, there can be no complaint if they do not exercise this in the manner that others might wish.

A simple form of trust may arise, where money is held in the name of another person who acknowledges, whether formally or informally, the true ownership. This is only suitable for relatively small sums of money because tax and other complications can arise.

It is possible for an elderly person prior to, but in the expectation of, becoming mentally incapable to transfer all money and assets to trustees under the terms of a settlement, whereby the trustees continue to manage the trust fund for the support and benefit of that person.

TYPES OF TRUSTS

Express Trust

This is the most common form of trust. In an express trust the subject matter and the object of the trust are clearly expressed. An express trust will usually provide instructions as to exactly how distributions are to be made for a named beneficiary or beneficiaries.

Discretionary Trust

A discretionary trust gives discretion to the trustees regarding how much of the trust fund is distributed, i.e. whether there is a capital sum distributed or whether all or part of the income from the capital is distributed. The discretionary trust will usually provide the trustees with the discretion to make distributions to one or more beneficiaries named in the trust at such times and in such amounts as the trustees think fit.

For a person who wishes to make arrangements for a child or adult with a disability, a discretionary trust may be useful. If the child or beneficiary is receiving a means-tested payment, distributions from the discretionary trust can be tailored to ensure that any distributions from the trust are not means-tested.

Most trusts, in practice, are created by a will and are normally created for the benefit of young beneficiaries or for a beneficiary or beneficiaries who have a disability, a drinking or gambling problem or who may be irresponsible when it comes to money.

There are tax implications when trusts are created and when distributions are made from a trust to a beneficiary. Professional advice must be obtained in relation to the creation of trusts as well as any distributions from trustees to a beneficiary under the trust.

The Advantages of a Trust

The advantages of a trust are that trustees are self-perpetuating and may be given wide discretionary powers. There is no need to pay fees or produce annual accounts to the court and the financial authority of trustees cannot be questioned. Trusts may also be used to avoid means testing for welfare benefits and contributions to the cost of local authority services.

The Disadvantages of a Trust

The disadvantages are that trusts cannot be set up by someone who is already incapacitated and the trustees only have authority over money placed in a trust. There is inadequate supervision with little control over administration costs or the charges of professional trustees, and trustees have no obligation to consult or visit an incapacitated beneficiary and have no one to turn to for approval of their actions. Problems may arise over unspent income and tax repayments in the hands of the beneficiary. If the trustees are given discretion (and this may be desirable from many points of view), the exercise of this discretion cannot be questioned by or on behalf of the beneficiary.

COVENANTS

In certain circumstances, an individual may claim relief against an assessment to income tax if that person is making payments by way of a covenant to another person. In order to qualify for relief, there must be a legal obligation to covenant a sum of money for a period which is in excess of six years. The covenantor must not retain any control over the money covenanted. The advantage of the covenant is that those who pay tax at 44 per cent (from 6 April 2000) may use it to reduce their liability to tax while increasing the disposable income of another person. If that person pays tax at a lower rate a tax saving is realised. The laws relating to the making of covenants have been restricted in recent years. The only circumstances in which an older person can receive sums which are deductible from the covenantor's income are:

• if that individual is permanently incapacitated (mentally or physically)

- if that individual is over 65 years of age (limitations introduced by section 13 of the Finance Act 1993)

- through payments which are part of a maintenance agreement between separated spouses.

The covenantor can claim relief in respect of covenanted amounts which do not exceed 5 per cent of the covenantor's income. An exception to this 5 per cent ceiling arises with regard to persons who are permanently incapacitated due to physical or mental incapacity (this exception only applies with reference to deeds of covenant executed after 8 February 1995). The Revenue Commissioners also have the discretion to waive this 5 per cent limit in the case of hardship.

The recipient of a covenanted amount may be liable to pay income tax on the sum covenanted. It is important to note that sums covenanted to persons in receipt of a non-contributory pension or means-tested allowance may affect their entitlement to the allowance in question. Separate rules apply in relation to money covenanted to minors.

If an older relation requires additional income to live on, or to pay for a nursing home, a Deed of Covenant may be the most tax efficient method of achieving this result.

REFERENCES

Cretney, Stephen, *Enduring Power of Attorney* (Jordans, Bristol, England) 3rd edition, 1991.

Department of Justice, Equality and Law Reform, *Wards of Court: An Information Booklet* (Dublin) 1998.

McLaughlin, Nuala, "Wardship: A legal and Medical Perspective" *Medico-Legal Journal of Ireland* (1998) Vol. 4, No. 2.

Thurston, John, *Powers of Attorney: A Practical Guide* (Tolley, Surrey, England) 2nd edition, 1997.

Chapter Four

A Guide to Occupational and Personal Pensions

A GUIDE TO PENSIONS

Unless you make provisions for your retirement, you may find that your only income will be your social welfare pension. This may not be sufficient to maintain your standard of living. Pension schemes provide for a tax effective means of saving for retirement. There are certain legal requirements in relation to the type of scheme which will be discussed, including the basic relationship of employer/employee.

The main advantages of a pension scheme are as follows:

1. Pension schemes which qualify as "exempt approved schemes" under the Finance Act 1972 or Part 30 of the Taxes Consolidation Act 1997 have certain tax advantages, e.g. contributions to the pension scheme qualify for tax relief subject to limits.

2. No tax is paid on the income or gains of the pension scheme.

The combination of the above means that you can accumulate more substantial savings during your working life by using a pension scheme than you may achieve by investing elsewhere.

There are three sources of pensions:

1. **Occupational pensions**: provided through employers' sponsored pension schemes.

2. **State pensions**: contributory and non-contributory old age pensions.

3. **Personal pensions**: designed for the self-employed and for those in non-pensionable employment.

This chapter discusses occupational pension schemes and personal pensions.

OCCUPATIONAL PENSIONS

Benefits on Retirement

During his/her working life, an employee will usually pay a certain percentage of their salary into a pension fund. This is known as a contributory scheme. When the employee pays no contributions, it is called a non-contributory scheme. If your occupational pension scheme is approved by the Revenue Commissioners, there is tax relief on contributions of up to 15 per cent of gross salary, or 20 per cent if you are over 55. The most common benefit coming from occupational schemes is a pension payable by regular instalments after an individual's retirement. Pensions are paid under the PAYE system and taxed accordingly. Frequently, a portion of pension entitlement can be exchanged at retirement for a lump sum, which is not subject to tax. In the public sector, occupational pension schemes provide a separate lump sum (or gratuity) and pension benefits. The rules of schemes generally provide for pensions to be paid from a specified date, generally known as "normal pensionable age". In most occupations this can be any age between 60 and 70, the most common age being 65. Pension scheme rules may also provide for reduced pensions to be paid at an earlier date, and they make a special provision for early payment if retirement takes place due to ill health. The rules may also provide for "late" retirement, i.e. if retirement is deferred beyond the normal pensionable age specified in the rules.

CONTRIBUTIONS AND BENEFITS THAT APPLY TO OCCUPATIONAL SCHEMES

Both the employer and the employee can contribute to a pension scheme, within certain limits:

• the employer's ordinary annual contributions are allowed as an expense and are not taxable as a benefit in kind to the employee

• employees can claim tax relief on personal contributions to the scheme subject to certain limits

• to obtain approval of a scheme, the employer must be a contributor to the scheme.

The scheme can provide for:

• a pension of up to two-thirds of final remuneration at normal retirement age for a member who has completed ten or more years of service either with that employer or with some employer. Generally, 40 years of service is needed before a pension of 66.67 per cent is earned by most employees

- an option to take a tax-free lump sum on retirement of one and a half times the final remuneration. (The maximum allowed is 150 per cent of the final salary, provided that twenty years of service with that employer has been completed by retirement age)

- a life cover of up to four times the remuneration

- a spouse's pension of up to two-thirds of the employee's pension

- children's pensions payable until the youngest child reaches eighteen years of age or ceases full-time education

- the indexation of both the employee's pension and the spouse's pension

- early retirement.

Funded Occupational Schemes

Pension schemes in private firms and in commercial semi-state bodies are usually financed by setting aside funds during the working lifetime of the employees. These funds are (normally) placed in the control of trustees who hold and invest the funds under the terms of a trust deed. One of the conditions of obtaining Revenue approval for a scheme is that the scheme is established under irrevocable trusts. A trust means that property is held by one or more persons (the trustees) for the benefit of others (the beneficiaries) and for a specific purpose. In pension trusts, the purpose is to provide benefits for retirement and other purposes for employees of particular employers.

By creating a trust fund, the pension scheme becomes legally separate from the employer's business. Schemes set up in this way are usually exempt from income tax and capital gains tax.

Trustees of pension schemes are usually appointed by the employer who sets up the scheme. They are often directors or senior managers of the company. Sometimes a member of the scheme is appointed as trustee to represent the other members.

In addition to the trust deed there are rules, and these contain the essential details of the scheme as it affects employees, i.e. the contributions and the benefits.

Unfunded Occupational Schemes

Some schemes, such as public service schemes, operate on a pay as you go basis. In other words, the cost of paying the benefits to workers who have retired is paid out of revenue coming into the scheme in much the same way as salaries and wages of employees are paid. These schemes are known as unfunded schemes.

DEFINED BENEFIT SCHEMES AND DEFINED CONTRIBUTION SCHEMES

There are two basic types of occupational schemes: defined benefit schemes and defined contribution schemes.

Defined Benefit Schemes

These schemes clearly set out in their rules the members' entitlements on retirement. It is common for the scheme to grant one-sixtieth of the final salary for each year of service. Defined benefit schemes often deduct the member's State social welfare pension entitlement when calculating the pension due to a member on retirement, and this will be stated in the rules of the scheme.

The funding of defined benefit schemes is under the supervision of actuaries who estimate the contribution rate needed to secure the pension promised, and advise the trustees and the employer accordingly.

Defined Contribution Schemes

These are schemes in which the employer and the members contribute to the scheme at an agreed fixed rate. In these schemes the members' benefits on retirement will depend on the total amount contributed to the fund and the investment returns earned.

Defined contribution schemes often give members a quotation, which has a "target pension". This is to give members an idea of what pensions they can expect on retirement. It is based on achieving a certain growth rate per year (normally 10 per cent) and it is only by monitoring fund performance on a yearly basis that you will be able to see if you are on target for these figures. In the case of a defined contribution scheme, the money you have built up at retirement purchases your pension, but there can often be a significant difference between the pension different life offices will give you for the same money.

Additional Voluntary Contributions (AVCs)

Most pension schemes will allow employees to improve their retirement benefits by making additional voluntary contributions (AVCs). AVCs may be invested in the main scheme or in a separate scheme.

Limits on AVCs for Occupational Pensions

The total employee contributions allowed for tax purposes is 15 per cent of gross pay in any year. This is inclusive of any ordinary contributions made, subject to the following conditions:

- that the additional benefits secured by AVCs, when added to the benefits of the main scheme, must be within the approval limit set by the Revenue Commissioners

- that no more than five-sixths of the member's total benefits from all pension schemes with the employer may have been paid for by the member.

Changing Jobs

Payments made to a pension fund after 1991, by employees who have a minimum of five years of qualifying service, are preserved and can be transferred to a new company scheme or to an approved insurance policy or contract. With your contributions made before 1991, you can choose to take out what you put in less 25 per cent tax, subject to the rules of your scheme. However, when you opt to transfer to another scheme, the Revenue Commissioners require that you transfer the total value of your fund into the new scheme, and refunds of pre-1991 contributions are not permitted.

Leaving a Pension Scheme

If you are leaving your job or if you have been made redundant, there may be several options open to you regarding your pension. These should be detailed on the relevant documents of your scheme. If you have over five years of qualifying service, at least two of which are after 1 January 1991, you will be entitled to preserved benefits when you leave your job. A refund of contributions made to you by the scheme for service after 1 January 1991 is no longer allowed if you are entitled to preserved benefits. Subject to your own scheme rules, contributions paid by you before 1 January 1991, or after that date if there is no entitlement to preserved benefits, may be refunded, provided you are not transferring to another scheme.

Death

Occupational pension schemes usually pay some benefits to your survivors if you die before retirement, most commonly as a lump sum. This could be up to four times your salary on top of your contributions, plus interest. Many schemes also provide pensions for dependants in addition to lump sum benefits. If you die after retirement, payments to you and your family will stop unless your pension is guaranteed payable for a certain minimum time, such as five years. If death occurs before this timescale is up, payment can be received by your survivors in a tax-free lump sum.

Sometimes the scheme rules provide for a specific dependant's pension to be paid on your death after retirement. These benefits may be payable immediately on your death, even though a five year guarantee may still be in force or payment may begin after the five year guarantee expires.

What Information Must Trustees Give?

Pension scheme trustees must account to the members on how the scheme is run. Under the Pensions Act 1990 and regulations made under the Act, trustees must give members or employees likely to become members, their spouses, other scheme beneficiaries and trade unions the following information:

- details about the documents constituting the scheme, i.e. the legal documents that govern it

- basic information about the scheme, which is usually contained in an explanatory booklet or document

- details of personal benefit entitlements under the scheme, usually given in the form of a benefit statement.

Scheme Reports

Depending on the size of the scheme, there is a wide range of reports that trustees may also have to make available, some automatically and some on request.

You are entitled to a regular flow of information on the performance in relation to management of the fund. This includes the scheme's annual report, which details investment performance, the names of trustees and other people who provide services relating to the scheme.

Members of larger defined benefit schemes can ask for yearly audited accounts. Employees of defined benefit schemes can also get access to the actuary's report on the scheme. New members must be given basic information about the scheme within two months of joining. They can request information in writing about their own personal benefits.

PERSONAL PENSIONS

For many self-employed people in contracted work, personal pension plans are the only alternative to provide a pension.

Personal pension funds on retirement depend on the number and the amount of contributions made, as well as profits from the investment. Most people pay a set amount each month, but if you have any regular income, you could choose to pay a series of once-off single premiums or a lump sum investment.

It is up to you how your contributions are invested. You can choose between a wide range of unit-linked funds covering equities, property, gifts and cash. Managed funds are unit-linked funds that have a mix of these assets.

PERSONAL PENSION PLANS: CHANGES INTRODUCED IN THE FINANCE ACT 1999

General Provisions

The Revenue Commissioners have produced a booklet entitled *New Pension Options*, for the self-employed and directors of family companies. This explains the changes introduced in the Finance Act 1999. You can obtain copies of this booklet or further information by contacting your tax office or by telephoning the Central Telephone Information Office at 01 878 0000. Pension companies and fund managers should contact the Retirement Benefits District at 01 631 8920. The adddress is: Shelbourne House, Shelbourne Road, Dublin 4.

Until the Finance Act 1999 was passed, people retiring were required to set aside 75 per cent of their pension fund to buy a fixed-rate annuity that would provide a guaranteed income until they died. However, low interest rates meant that the amount of pension income they could buy was much lower than it was even a year previously.

Since the Finance Act 1999 was passed, major changes to pensions for the self-employed took effect on 6 April 1999. In relation to contributions, people up to the age of 30 are able to make contributions of up to 15 per cent of the net relevant earnings to pension plans. Between the ages of 30 and 40, the limit is 20 per cent, from the age of 40 to 50 there is a 25 per cent limit and for those aged over 50, up to 30 per cent of income may be contributed to the pension fund.

The new rules are explained in detail in the Revenue booklet entitled *New Pension Options for the Self-Employed and Directors of Family Companies, Booklet IT14.*

SPECIFIC PROVISIONS

The following is a summary of specific new arrangements for retirement provisions for the self-employed and others:

Maximum contributions: an earnings cap of £200,000 a year applies to the contribution limits. Therefore, the maximum contribution for an individual of 50 years and over is £60,000 (30 per cent of £200,000).

Transfer of funds during the pension accumulation period: individuals have the option of transferring their funds accumulated with one insurer to another fund with another insurer.

Ownership of the fund on retirement: on retirement, the individual can opt for either the existing (annuity) arrangement or the alternative new option (set out below). Under the new option, the fund is the property of the individual and on death, his/her estate. Income tax or inheritance tax can apply in the event of death and legal advice is required for more information.

Triggering the pension: the old legislation provided that an individual must have exercised the option to take a pension between the ages of 60 and 70 years of age. The age limit of 70 years has been increased to 75.

New options: 25 per cent of the accumulated pension fund is available as a tax-free lump sum. An individual can, however, opt for a lower entitlement than 25 per cent.

If the pensioner already has a guaranteed income for life of £10,000 through pension or annuity, his/her pension fund can be transferred to an approved retirement fund (ARF). This can be any fund operated by a bank, building society, credit union or insurance company. It will be up to the individual to choose his/her own investment.

The pensioner will also be able to withdraw money from this fund as and when he/she chooses and could even withdraw the whole amount. If, however, he/she does not have the minimum of £10,000 annual income, he/she will be required to place £50,000 of the pension fund into an approved minimum retirement fund (AMRF). The money in the AMRF cannot fall below £50,000 until he/she reaches the age of 75, after which it can be withdrawn.

PENSIONS BOARD

The Pensions Board was established by the Minister for Social Welfare under the terms of the Pensions Act 1990. Its main functions are:

- to monitor and supervise the operation of the Pensions Act and pension developments generally

- to issue guidelines on the duties and responsibilities of the trustees of schemes and codes of practice on specific aspects of the irresponsibilities

- to encourage the provision of appropriate training for trustees of schemes and to advise the Minister on standards for trustees

- to advise the Minister on the operation of the Pensions Act and on pension matters generally.

Pension schemes must register with the Pensions Board and most schemes must pay an annual fee to meet the Board's administrative costs. The Board can act on behalf of pension scheme members who are concerned about their scheme. It can investigate the operation of pension schemes, has the power to prosecute for breaches of the Pensions Act and to take court actions against trustees for the protection of members and their rights.

The Pensions Board includes representatives of trade unions, employers, government, member trustees, the pensions industry and the various professional groups involved with occupational pension schemes.

FURTHER INFORMATION

A number of booklets are available free of charge from the Pensions Board:

1. *What Do You Know About Your Pension Scheme?*: an overview of the information which trustees of occupational pension schemes must give.

2. *Is My Pension Secure?*: a guide to the protections provided by the Pensions Act, designed specifically for members.

3. *Selecting Member Trustees*: a guide to the participation by members in the selection of the trustees of occupational pension schemes.

4. *So You Are a Pension Scheme Trustee*: a brief guide to the duties and responsibilities of trustees of occupational pension schemes.

5. *The Pensions Board*: an introduction to the board, its functions and its membership.

6. *What Happens to My Pension if I Leave?*: a guide to the preservation and transfer of benefits for early leavers under the Pensions Act.

7. *A Brief Guide to the Pension Provisions of the Family Law Acts*: guidance on the pension provisions of the Family Law Act 1995 and the Family Law Divorce Act 1996.

8. *What Happens when Your Pension Scheme Is Wound Up or a Merger/ Acquisition Takes Place?*: a guide to trustees and pension scheme members on the winding up of a pensions scheme and on the effects of mergers/acquisitions on pension schemes.

9. *A Guide to Your Scheme's Annual Report*: a guide for pension scheme members to assist them in reading and understanding their scheme's annual report.

10. *A Brief Guide to Pensions*: a guide to help you understand your pension scheme and benefits.

11. *Securing Retirement Income — National Pensions' Policy Initiative*: a brief guide to the report of the Pensions Board.

The address of the Pensions Board is:
Holbrook House
Holles Street
Dublin 2
Tel. 01 676 2622; Fax. 01 676 4714.

Chapter 5

State and Health Board Income Support for Older or Retired People

INTRODUCTION

Benefits for Older People

Apart from a free travel pass for which everyone over 66 qualifies, there are very few universal benefits for older people. There are, on the other hand, a very large number of payments, grants, types of pensions, benefits and special concessions available from many sources, for which persons may be eligible.

Social Welfare and Health Board Payments

These include social insurance payments which are based on your pay-related social insurance (PRSI) contributions and means-tested payments if your income is below a certain level. If you are not entitled to a payment based on your insurance contributions, you may apply for a means-tested payment from the Department of Social, Community and Family Affairs or the health board.

Rates of Payment

In the case of social insurance payments, the maximum rates are paid to those who satisfy the qualifying standards in terms of contributions paid and/or credited in the appropriate insurance classes. The minimum rates are paid if you have just enough contributions to qualify. In the case of means-tested payments, the maximum rates are paid if you have little or no means, but it is possible to have some savings and still qualify for some level of payment.

PRSI Contributions

There are various conditions attached to many of the cash payments. The following are the most important:

Insurance rates: there are different rates of insurance. Most benefits are available to those insured at the full rate of PRSI, typically if you work in the private sector. Most public servants pay a lower rate of PRSI and are eligible only for the Widow's/Orphan's Pension and Bereavement Grant. Since April 1995, new entrants to the public service pay full PRSI, Class A.

Mixed contributions: if you have paid both a full and modified rate, you may qualify for a mixed insurance pro rata retirement or old age pension. Contributions paid in another EU State, or a country with which Ireland has a bilateral social security agreement, may qualify for benefit or pension under EU rules.

Self-employment: most self-employed people began to pay PRSI in 1988. Many are now eligible for the Widow's Contributory Pension and qualify for old age pension from 1998. If you paid contributions (either employed or voluntary) before 1988, you may qualify earlier.

Self-employed people pay PRSI at the Class S rate, which entitles them to the Contributory Old Age Pension, Widow's/Widower's Pensions, Maternity and Adoptive Benefit and Bereavement Grant, subject to fulfilling the necessary conditions.

Credited contributions: if you retire before the age of 65, you must take steps to keep your contributions up to date.

Means test: means tests for non-contributory payments are complex and your income from virtually all sources is taken into account. The house you live in is not counted as means unless you get an income from it, such as letting some rooms. In general, you cannot give away money or property in order to get a pension, as it may still be counted as means. There is one exception to this — you may give a farm up to a certain rateable valuation to a child if he/she intends to work the farm.

If you or your spouse are over 66 and you sell your house in order to provide alternative accommodation or to pay nursing home fees, some of the proceeds from the sale may not, under certain circumstances, be taken into account for the purpose of determining means. However, this exemption will not apply if you move in with family or friends instead of buying a new home or flat.

Dependants: if you qualify for a social welfare or health board weekly payment, you will generally receive extra amounts for adult and child dependants. An adult dependant can be a spouse or non-marital partner. Children up to eighteen years of age and living at home are normally regarded as dependants. Young adults up to the age of 22 and in full-time education are usually classed as dependants. An adult dependant receiving a social welfare or health board payment in their own right or with an income of £60 or more a week is not regarded as a dependant.

December 1999 Budget

In most cases, this Budget increased the weekly rates of Social Insurance or Assistance from May 2000. See Tables 1–3 at the end of this chapter for the increases that will apply.

Pensions and Allowances for Older People

There are three personal pensions payable through the social welfare system. These are paid from the age of 66 to qualified contributors who have retired. These are the Retirement Pension, the Contributory Old Age Pension and the Non-Contributory Old Age Pension. You may receive only one social welfare pension at a time. In addition, there are a number of allowances for older people.

RETIREMENT PENSION

You will qualify for a Retirement Pension if you are aged 65, are retired from full-time employment or if you satisfy certain PRSI contribution conditions. It is not necessary to give up employment completely. You can be in part-time employment and earn less than £30 per week paying PRSI Class J or earn less than £2,500 per year if you are self-employed.

The retirement condition no longer applies on reaching the age of 66. In order to receive the retirement pension, you must have started paying PRSI before reaching the age of 55, have at least 156 weeks PRSI paid and have a yearly average of at least 48 weeks PRSI paid or credited from 1979 to the end of the tax year before you reach the age of 65. This will entitle you to a maximum pension (this applies only if you reach the age of 65 on or after 6 April 1992). A yearly average of at least 24 weeks PRSI paid or credited from 1953 (or the time you started insurable employment, if later) to the end of the tax year before you reach the age of 65, will entitle you to the minimum pension.

A yearly average of 24 weeks PRSI paid or credited will entitle you to a minimum rate of Retirement Pension. For the maximum pension, an average of 48 weeks PRSI is needed.

Rates of Payment

The maximum rate of Retirement Pension effective from June 1999 is a weekly rate of £89 and £96 from May 2000 (provided for in the 1 December 1999 Budget). An extra £5.00 is payable if you are 80 or over.

OLD AGE CONTRIBUTORY PENSION

For an Old Age Contributory Pension, you must have:

- started paying PRSI before reaching the age of 56

- at least 156 weeks PRSI paid (260 weeks full rate PRSI paid are needed if the yearly average is between ten and nineteen)

- a yearly average of at least 48 weeks PRSI paid or credited from 1979 to the end of the tax year before you reach the age of 66. This will entitle you to a maximum pension (this applies only if you reached the age of 66 on or after 6 April 1992)

- a yearly average of at least ten weeks PRSI paid and/or credited from 1953 (or the time you commenced insurable employment, if later) to the end of the tax year before you reach the age of 66. This will entitle you to the minimum rate of Old Age (Contributory) Pension.

Rates of Payment

The maximum rate of Old Age Contributory Pension effective from June 1999 is a weekly rate of £89, and £96 from May 2000 (provided for in 1 December 1999 Budget). An extra £5.00 is payable if you are 80 or over.

Additional Allowances Payable with a Retirement Pension or Old Age Contributory Pension

Your pension is made up of a personal rate for yourself. You may also receive extra amounts, e.g. an increase in respect of a qualified adult and/ or a child dependant, a Living Alone Allowance (if you are aged 66 or over and living entirely alone) and a Fuel Allowance. Also, on reaching the age of 80 most pensions increase by £5 per week.

Qualified Adult Allowance

If your spouse (or cohabiting partner) does not have an income of £60 or more per week (i.e. £3,120 or more per year), you are entitled to claim a Qualified Adult Allowance in respect of him/her if he/she is dependent on you. His/her income from most sources (e.g. employment, property rental, self-employment, occupational pensions etc.) as well as any savings or investments he/she has are taken into account in calculating the total amount of the income.

As regards savings/investments, the following formula is applied in order to establish the yearly income:

- the first £2,000 of the savings and investments is ignored
- the next £20,000 is assessed at 7.5 per cent
- the remainder is assessed at 15 per cent.

Based on this formula, savings/investments of £32,800 work out at £60 per week.

Dependent Child Allowance

If you have one child or more who is residing with you and is financially dependent on you, you may claim Dependent Child Allowance as part of your pension. This is payable at the rate of £15.20 per week in respect of each child under the age of 18. The allowance is also payable if the child is aged between 18 and 22 and he/she is in full-time education. In the latter case, certification of attendance from the school or college is required. The rates of Old Age Contributory Pension are as follows:

Yearly average insurance contributions up to 1999	Rates from June 1999
48 and over	89.00
36–47	86.60
24–35	83.70
20–23	81.90
15–19	66.80
10–14	44.50

As outlined above, your personal rate of pension is based on your average social insurance contribution record over the period of your working life. Note: The maximum rate of £89 has been increased to £96 from May 2000 in the December 1999 Budget.

The Qualified Adult Allowance for Retirement and Old Age (Contributory) Pensions is as follows:

	From June 1999
Qualified Adult under age 66	£55.50
Qualified Adult age 66 and over	£59.90

The Dependent Child Allowance rates are £15.20 (full-rate) or £7.60 (half-rate) per child per week.

PENSION ARRANGEMENTS FOR THE SELF-EMPLOYED

A special Old Age (Contributory) Pension has been introduced from 9 April 1999 for self-employed people who were 56 years of age or over on 6 April 1988, when social insurance was extended to self-employed people. These people fail to qualify for a pension under existing rules.

Qualifying Conditions

To qualify for this pension, a person must:

• have been aged 56 or over on 6 April 1988 (that is, born on or before 6 April 1932)

• have started paying PRSI contributions as a self-employed person on or after 6 April 1988

• have a minimum of 260 weeks (five years) PRSI contributions paid on a compulsory basis since 6 April 1988.

Rates of Payment

Payment will be made at 50 per cent of the maximum standard Old Age (Contributory) Pension rate. The personal rates of payment are £41.50 from 9 April 1999 and £44.50 from 4 June 1999.

In certain circumstances, a qualified adult allowance is payable in respect of a dependent spouse/partner. This allowance is payable at the following rates:

	From 4 June 1999
Spouse/partner under age 66	£27.80
Spouse/partner age 66 or over	£30.00

A Dependent Child Allowance is payable in respect of children up to the age of 18, or the age of 22 if in full-time education. This allowance is payable at £7.60 a week for each child.

Implementation Arrangements

Entitlement to this pension exists from 9 April 1999. However, due to the administrative effort required to process the claim load involved, payment commenced on 15 October 1999. Arrears, where due, will also be paid at this time.

Refunds of PRSI Contributions

A person who was 56 years of age or over when they first started paying PRSI as a self-employed person and does not qualify for either an Old Age (Contributory) or (Non-Contributory) Pension can receive a refund of the pension element (53 per cent) of his/her paid PRSI contributions (with interest). This facility will remain in place for anyone who does not qualify under the new pension arrangements.

Important Note

Self-employed persons who previously applied for an Old Age (Contributory) Pension but were unsuccessful will be contacted by the pension services office and advised regarding entitlement.

Further Information

If you would like further information, advice and/or a claim form, you can phone 01 7043351 or 071 69800, or you can contact the Pension Services Office, College Road, Sligo. Alternatively, you may apply for the new pension by completing an Old Age (Contributory) Pension claim form (RP/CP1). This form is available from your local Social Welfare Office or post office.

OLD AGE NON-CONTRIBUTORY PENSION

You will qualify for an Old Age Non-Contributory Pension if you are aged 66 or over and you are living in the State and satisfy a means test. The Non-Contributory Pension is payable to people who do not have enough contributions to qualify for a Contributory Pension and who satisfy a means test.

Your pension is made up of a personal rate for yourself plus increases for any persons who are living with you and financially dependent on you (e.g. a dependent spouse/partner or a dependent child). The current maximum personal rate of Old Age Non-Contributory Pension is £78.50 per week (£85.50 per week from May 2000), for those under 80 years of age. Your payment will be increased automatically by £5 per week on reaching the age of 80.

Qualified Adult Allowance

If your spouse (or cohabiting partner) is under the age of 66, you are entitled to claim a Qualified Adult Allowance in respect of him/her if he/she is dependent on you. This allowance currently amounts to £44.20 per week at the maximum rate. (£51.70 per week from May 2000.)

> Note: Once your spouse/partner reaches 66 years of age, he/she is entitled to claim an Old Age Pension in his/her own right. If he/she does qualify for a pension, then the Qualified Adult Allowance is no longer payable to you.

Dependent Child Allowance

If you have children who are residing with you and who are financially dependent on you, you may claim Dependent Child Allowance as part of your pension. This is payable at the rate of £13.20 per week in respect of each child under the age of 18. The allowance is also payable if the child is aged between 18 and 22 and he/she is in full-time education. In the latter case, certification of attendance from the school or college is required.

Means Test

Your means are any income you or your spouse/partner have, or property (except your home) or other asset, which could provide you with an income. The main items which are counted as means include:

- cash income, e.g. earnings from employment or self-employment (including income from farming) or another pension (including social security pensions from another country), etc.

> - the value of any property you or your spouse/partner have (but not your own home)
> - the value of any investments and capital you or your spouse/partner have.

How Investments, Property and Capital Are Assessed

The actual income from investments and money held by you and/or your spouse/partner is not how your means is calculated. Instead, the investment items are added together and a formula is used to work out your means. The formula, which is displayed below, only applies up to October 2000.

Formula:

If you are single or widowed:

- the first £2,000 is ignored
- the next £20,000 is calculated at 7.5 per cent
- the balance over £22,000 is calculated at 15 per cent.

If you are married or cohabiting:

- the first £4,000 is ignored
- the next £40,000 is calculated at 7.5 per cent
- the balance over £44,000 is calculated at 15 per cent.

This gives a yearly value, which is divided by 52 to give the weekly means.

If you are single or widowed, you can get the minimum rate of pension even if you have savings up to £40,430 and have no other means. If you are married or cohabiting you can get the minimum rate of pension even if you have savings up to £80,860 and have no other means. You will still get a full pension if you have savings or investments up to £6,160 (for single and widowed) and £12,320 (for married or cohabiting) and have no other means. You will now see from this that you can have savings between the amounts shown and still get a reduced rate of pension, if you have no other means. After October 13, 2000 a single/widowed person and a married person will receive the full pension if they have savings or investments less than £16,000 and £32,000 respectively.

October 2000 Changes

The rules for calculating means attributable to such capital with regard to claimants for the Old Age Non-Contributory Pension, Blind Pension, Widow(er)'s Non-Contributory Pension and Carer's Allowance, are being changed from October 2000 to the following:

1. The first £10,000 is ignored.

2. The weekly value of the next £10,000 (from £10,000 to £20,000) is assessed at £1 per £1,000.

3. The weekly value of the next £10,000 (from £20,000 to £30,000) is assessed at £2 per £1,000.

4. The weekly value of capital over £30,000 is assessed at £4 per £1,000.

Reduced Rate Old Age Non-Contributory Pension

If your weekly means are over £6.00 and under £82.00, you will qualify for a reduced rate of Old Age Non-Contributory Pension. There are several reduced rates of pension, depending on the person's weekly means. Every £2.00 of weekly means over £6.00 reduces the rate of pension by £2.00 for a single or widowed person and it also reduces the rate for a qualified adult dependant by £1.00 per week.

Items Exempt from Means Test

Farm Retirement Scheme: if you receive payment from the Department of Agriculture and Food under the Farm Retirement Scheme it is not assessed as means. However, this retirement payment may be reduced by the amount of your Old Age Non-Contributory Pension.

Sale of residence: if you sell your own home after the age of 66, to move to more suitable accommodation, the proceeds of the sale of your house up to £75,000 may be exempted from your means in certain circumstances. This would apply where you buy another suitable house, rent alternative accommodation, or move into a nursing home.

Disregard from earnings: if you are working and have dependent children, £104 per year or £2 per week for each dependent child is not counted as means.

PRE-RETIREMENT ALLOWANCE

If you are aged 55 or over and are getting long-term Unemployment Assistance, this allowance allows you to retire from the labour market and receive a weekly allowance instead of Unemployment Assistance. This means that you will no longer have to sign on.

You will qualify if you:

- are aged 55 years or over
- have been receiving Unemployment Benefit/Assistance for at least 390 days
- are no longer entitled to one-parent family payment or Carer's Allowance
- are separated from your spouse and have not worked or been self-employed in the last fifteen months
- satisfy a means test
- retire from the workforce
- are living in the State.

Rates of Payment

The rates applying from June 1999 are:

1. A weekly rate of £73.50.

2. An additional sum for a qualified adult of £43.20.

3. An additional sum for each dependent child of £13.20 (full rate), £6.60 (half rate).

EU FARM RETIREMENT SCHEME

Details of the Scheme

The EU Farm Retirement Scheme provides for the early retirement of farmers in the 55–66 age group and the transfer of land to farmers in the 18–50 age group. Farmers who retire receive a retirement pension. The details of the scheme are set out in the *Scheme for Early Retirement from Farming,* published by the Minister for Agriculture and Food (Agriculture House, Kildare Street, Dublin 2).

In order to qualify under the scheme, the retiring farmer must, on the date he/she ceases farming (i.e. the date on which the transfer documents are signed) be between 55 and 66 and must have at least five hectares of land and have practised farming as a main occupation for the preceding ten years.

On the date of the transfer, the person receiving the farm must:

- be under 50 years of age

- have been engaged in farming for at least three years and have appropriate qualifications in agriculture or horticulture if born after 1 January, or if born before 1 January 1968 have been engaged in farming for at least five years, or otherwise have acceptable qualifications

- take over as head of the agricultural holding, which must have at least five hectares

- subsequently expand the holding by at least five hectares or 10 per cent whichever is the greater

- own or lease at least five hectares which were not transferred on or after 30 July 1992 and take over all or at least five hectares or 10 per cent of the land released by the retiring farmer, whichever is the greater, in order to expand his land

- undertake to practise farming as a main occupation for at least five years or for as long as the early retirement pension is payable and the farm is in harmony with the requirements of EU and national legislation on environmental protection.

The rate of the annual pension is a basic 4,000 ECUS per year and 250 ECUS per hectare, up to a maximum of 10,000 ECUS for a farm of 24 hectares or more. The pension is paid for ten years or until the retiring farmer's seventieth birthday, whichever is the shorter.

The Farm Retirement Pension is reduced by the amount of any old age or retirement pension received from the Department of Social, Community and Family Affairs.

There is also a pension scheme for workers or family helpers between their fiftieth and sixtieth birthdays, who lose their employment as a result of the farmer's early retirement.

> Note: This scheme is due to be replaced by new EU legislation later this year (2000).

WIDOW'S/WIDOWER'S CONTRIBUTORY PENSION

From 20 October 1994, widowers have the same contributory pension entitlements as widows. You will qualify if:

- you are widowed

- you are not cohabiting

- your late spouse was in receipt of either a Retirement Pension or an Old Age Contributory Pension with an entitlement to an increase for you

- you satisfy the following PRSI contribution conditions based on your late spouse's or your own PRSI contributions (Classes A, B, C, D, H and S):
  (a) at least 156 weeks PRSI paid to the date your spouse died
  (b) either an average of 39 weeks PRSI paid or credited over the three or five tax years before he/she died or reached pension age
  (c) if a yearly average of at least 24 weeks PRSI has been paid or credited since starting work up to the end of the tax year before he/she died or reached pension age a minimum pension can be obtained. In order to obtain a maximum pension, 48 weeks are needed.

Rates of Payment

From May 2000, the rates are as follows:

1. Under the age of 66: £81.10.

2. Aged 66 and under the age of 80: £89.10.

3. Aged 80 and over: £94.10.

WIDOW'S/WIDOWER'S NON-CONTRIBUTORY PENSION

If you are a widow/widower and not entitled to a survivor's Contributory Pension, you may be entitled to a survivor's Non-Contributory Pension. You will qualify if you:

- are widowed

- are not cohabiting

- satisfy a means test

- are living in the State.

Rates of Payment

The rate of widow's/widower's Non-Contributory Pension from May 2000 is:

1. Aged under 66: £77.50 per week.

2. Aged over 66: £85.50 per week.

3. Aged 80 and over: £90.50 per week.

4. Additional Living Alone Allowance (aged under 66): nil.

5. Additional Living Alone Allowance (aged over 66): £6 per week.

Special Grant

From 1 December 1999, a special additional grant of £1,000 will be paid to widows/widowers with dependent children following the death of their spouse. This grant is in addition to the Bereavement Grant.

Allowances for Older People

Aged 80 Allowance: the Old Age Contributory Pension is increased in May 2000 from £96 to £101 per week when the pensioner reaches the age of 80.

Living Alone Allowance: the allowance is paid to anyone aged 66 or over who is receiving any Irish social welfare pension and is living alone. This payment is £6 per week. You must apply separately for this allowance.

PAYMENTS ARISING FROM A DEATH

There are a number of payments which may be made to survivors and/or dependants when someone dies:

Bereavement Grants

A Bereavement Grant of £500 applies in relation to persons who died on or after 2 February 1999, provided the deceased had at least 156 weeks PRSI paid since entering into insurable employment or has satisfied certain other conditions. For further information contact: Bereavement Grant Section, Social Welfare Services Office, Government Buildings, Ballinalee Road, Longford or telephone: 043 45211 (for Dublin callers 704 3487).

When the Social Welfare Office is notified of the death of a pensioner or his/her dependants, they will issue an application form for the Bereavement Grant to the next of kin. Alternatively, claim forms are available from any post office, Social Welfare Office or by contacting the Old Age Non-Contributory Pension's section in the Sligo Office. The deceased person's Death Certificate together with the funeral bill or receipt of payment should be sent along with the claim. The Bereavement Grant is normally payable to the person responsible for the payment of the funeral bill.

Payments after the Death of the Recipient

To qualify for payment after the death of the recipient, either the claimant or an adult dependant of the claimant must have been receiving certain social welfare or health board payments. If applicable, the payment continues for six weeks after the death. Equally, an Adult Dependant's Allowance or a Carer's Allowance can, under certain circumstances, be paid for six weeks after the death.

If your spouse/partner is getting an Old Age Contributory or Retirement Pension in his/her own right and you die, the Social Welfare will pay your spouse/partner the married rate of Old Age Contributory or Retirement pension for six weeks following the death.

If your spouse/partner is getting Old Age Non-Contributory Pension in his/her own right and you die, the Social Welfare will pay your spouse/partner both pensions for a period of six weeks following the death.

If your spouse/partner is getting a Carer's Allowance for looking after you and you die, the Social Welfare will pay your pension at the married rate (but not the Carer's Allowance) to your spouse/partner for six weeks following your death. It is very important therefore, that the Social Welfare are notified of the death of a social welfare pensioner or his/her qualified adult as soon as possible. If your pension is being paid by electronic fund transfer, it is not sufficient for the financial institution into which the pension is being paid to be notified of the death.

ADDITIONAL PAYMENTS

There are a number of health board payments for people who are trying to manage on a very low income or have little or no means. These include supplementary welfare allowances and assistance with rent or mortgage.

Supplementary Welfare Allowance (SWA): to qualify, you need to be trying to manage on a very low income or have insufficient means. The weekly allowance is paid to provide a basic minimum income. You may also qualify for a weekly supplement towards rent, food and heat. An exceptional need payment may also be available to meet a particular problem such as rent or mortgage, buying household equipment, school clothing and footwear or meeting funeral expenses. Emergency payments may be made following tragedies or accidents. Full details about SWA are available from the Community Welfare Officer at your local health centre.

Rent or Mortgage Assistance: to qualify, you need to be totally dependent on a social welfare payment, but this is a discretionary scheme under the supplementary welfare allowance so there is no absolute right to assistance.

Payment when someone is ill or needs care: there are a number of payments available to families or individuals who need or give care or who cannot work due to illness or disability. These include a Carer's Allowance, Disability Benefit, Disability Allowance, Invalidity Pension, Blind Pension, Blind Welfare Allowance, Mobility Allowance and various allowances or concessions for disabled drivers.

Disability Benefit (to be renamed "Sickness Benefit"): you must be aged under 66 and be incapable of work due to illness. You must have had a certain amount of social insurance contributions. You must notify the department within seven days of becoming ill and send in a medical certificate during each week of your illness. No payment is made for the first three days of illness. It remains payable for up to a year if you continue to be ill. After that, it may continue to be payable if you have at least 260 weeks (i.e. five years) PRSI contributions paid.

Disability Allowance (formerly DPMA): this is a means-tested payment made by the Department of Social, Community and Family Affairs to people with a disability who are aged between 16 and 66. It replaced the DPMA in October 1996. The disability must be likely to last at least twelve months.

Invalidity Pension (to be renamed "Disability Pension"): you may get this if you have been receiving Disability (Sickness) Benefit for at least twelve months and have 260 weeks PRSI contributions on your record.

Carer's Allowance: the Carer's Allowance is a payment for carers on low incomes who live with and look after certain people who need full-time care and attention. Carers who are providing care to more than one person may be entitled to up to 50 per cent extra of the maximum rate of

Carer's Allowance each week, depending on the weekly means assessed.

You will qualify if you, the carer:

- are aged eighteen or over
- satisfy a means test
- live with the person(s) you are looking after or live very close to them
- are caring for the person(s) on a full-time basis
- are not employed or self-employed outside the home for more than ten hours per week (August 1999)
- are living in the State
- are not living in a hospital, convalescent home or other similar institution.

The person you are caring for must be:
- so disabled as to need full-time care and attention
- not normally living in a hospital, home or other similar institution
- aged 66 or over.

From May 2000, the Carer's Allowance for a person under the age of 66 will be £80.50 per week and £85.50 per week for someone aged 66 and over. Since June 1999, it is also possible to obtain an annual payment of £200 towards the cost of respite care. Since April 1999, all carers of people receiving constant attendance or prescribed relative allowance have qualified for a free travel pass in their own right. There are also certain additional benefits for carers applying since August 1999:

1. **Blind Pension**: to qualify, you must be eighteen years of age or over, be blind and satisfy a means test. You may also qualify for the Blind Welfare Allowance.

2. **Blind Welfare Allowance (health board payment)**: to qualify, you must be blind, regarded as unemployable and satisfy a means test. This is a health board payment operated in conjunction with the National Council for the Blind, 45 Whitworth Road, Drumcondra, Dublin 9 (Tel. 01 8307033).

3. **Mobility Allowance (health board payment)**: to qualify, you must have a severe disability that renders you unable to work but able to benefit from a change of surroundings. You must satisfy a means test

and the strict medical criteria for eligibility.

4. **Payment for disabled driver/passengers (health board payment)**: to qualify, you must be disabled and need to buy and adapt a car in order to get to work. There are grants available from the health board to help you with such costs.

5. **Free Electricity/TA Allowances**: from October 2000 carers will receive the free electricity and TV allowances.

FREE SCHEMES

This is the name given to the package of benefits to which you may be entitled if you receive a payment from the Social Welfare or a health board payment and are aged 66 or over. The benefits in kind include free travel, electricity, gas and fuel allowance, free colour television licence and more.

Note: From October 2000, people aged 75 years of age and over, will be entitled to the Free Electricity Allowance, Free Telephone Rental Allowance and Full Television Licence, regardless of their circumstances.

The following information on free schemes is taken from the Department of Social, Community and Family Affairs Newsletter for Pensioners (1999).

FREE TRAVEL

You are entitled to a Free Travel Pass if you are aged 66 or over and permanently resident in the State.

Who Can Accompany You Free of Charge?

If you qualify for free travel, then you will receive a particular type of Free Travel Pass which allows your spouse (or a person with whom you are living as husband or wife) to accompany you free of charge when travelling.

Regardless of marital status, you may qualify for a Companion Free Travel Pass. This is a special type of pass, which entitles you and any one other person aged sixteen or over, to travel free of charge with you. You may qualify for this type of travel pass if you are unable to travel unaccompanied for medical reasons.

What Are Your Free Travel Entitlements?

Your Free Travel Pass entitles you to travel free on the road and rail services of the CIE group of companies (Bus Átha Cliath, Iarnród Éireann and Bus Éireann) and also on the transport services provided by another 54 private bus operators and sixteen private ferry operators throughout the country. Most pass holders may travel on the Aer Arran airline service between Co. Galway and the Aran Islands, at a specially reduced price. Certain restrictions apply on CIE services. These are indicated below.

Service	Times when free travel is NOT available
Bus Átha Cliath (Dublin Bus)	Monday to Friday inclusive 7.00 a.m. to 9.45 a.m. 4.30 p.m. to 6.30 p.m.
Bus Éireann (provincial city services in Cork and Limerick Cities)	Monday to Friday inclusive 7.00 a.m. to 9.45 a.m. 4.30 p.m. to 6.30 p.m.
Bus Éireann (Long distance services)	Fridays from 4.00 p.m. to 7.00 p.m. within a twenty mile radius of Dublin, Cork and Limerick.

Also, free travel is not available on a number of other CIE services. Such services include excursion and special bus or rail services, organised group journeys, Bus Átha Cliath NITELINK and special airport services, as well as First Class or Super Class travel on any service not listed in the official rail and bus timetables of the CIE group of companies.

Since 1999, anyone aged 75 years or over who is medically unfit to travel alone is eligible for a Companion Free Travel Pass. The new pass allows the applicant to have a person aged sixteen years or over to accompany the applicant while travelling on public transport and with certain private transport operators who participate in the Free Travel Scheme. Applications are made to: Over 75 Companion Pass Section, Pension Services Office, College Road, Sligo (Tel. 071 69800, ext. 8345 or 01 704 3345).

Free Cross-Border Travel

You may use your travel pass to undertake cross-border journeys to Northern Ireland and vice versa. Your journey must originate in one jurisdiction and terminate in the other jurisdiction. There are particular transport operators who provide this service (e.g. Iarnród Éireann, Bus Éireann, Ulsterbus, Northern Ireland Railways as well as several private bus operators). This free cross-boarder travel service is also available to people aged 65 or over who reside in Northern Ireland who hold a Northern Ireland Concession Travel Pass.

FREE ELECTRICITY ALLOWANCE (FREE TO ALL PEOPLE AGED OVER 75 FROM OCTOBER 2000)

As you are getting a social welfare pension, you may be eligible to receive a Free Electricity Allowance from the department. Alternatively, you may be entitled to a Free Natural Gas Allowance, Free Bottled Gas Refill Allowance or Free Electricity (Group Account) Allowance. Only one allowance is payable per household. If you qualify for any of these allowances, you automatically qualify for a free colour television licence when your current licence becomes due for renewal.

If you choose to receive either the Free Electricity or the Free Natural Gas Allowance, it is important to ensure that the electricity or gas meter account in your home is in your own name. This is to enable the ESB or Bord Gáis to credit the allowance to your account. If you are aged 75 or over and do not live in a hospital or other institution, you will qualify for whichever of these benefits you choose, regardless of who resides with you or where you live. For instance, if you live in the home of your son or daughter or another person, you will qualify for the allowance provided the gas or electricity account of the residence in question is in your own name.

If you are between 66 and 75, you must live either entirely alone or only with certain other people. Such people may include:

- a person for whom you are getting a Qualified Adult Allowance as part of your social welfare pension

- dependants under the age of 18 or under the age of 22 if in full-time education

- a disabled person

- another person who would qualify for the allowance in their own right, e.g. a person getting Old Age Contributory or Retirement Pension

- a person who provides you, or another person living with you with full-time care and attention if you or that other person is disabled.

The Free Electricity Allowance covers the normal standing charges on your electricity meter. It also provides you with 1,500 units of free electricity each year (i.e. 300 units in each of the three winter electricity billing periods and 200 units in each of the three summer periods). If you do not use up your free units in a billing period, you may carry forward your unused units for use in later periods. In fact, you can accumulate and carry forward up to 600 units.

If you also have a Nightsaver meter, you can choose to have your unused free units offset against the electricity usage on that meter. This offset is done by the ESB once a year — usually before the beginning of winter.

FREE NATURAL GAS ALLOWANCE

If you live in Dublin, Cork, Limerick, Waterford, Kilkenny, Tipperary or Clonmel, your home may be connected to a natural gas supply. If so, you may choose to receive the Free Natural Gas Allowance instead of the electricity allowance.

If you pay for natural gas on the Standard Rate Tariff, the allowance will cover:

- a supply charge of £22 and up to £5 of free natural gas in each of the two monthly billing periods of winter

- a credit of £18 against your overall natural gas bill in each of the two monthly billing periods of summer.

Alternatively, if you pay for natural gas on the Reducing Tariff, the allowance will cover:

- the normal standing charge and up to 498 kWhs in each of the two monthly billing periods of winter

- the normal standing charge and up to 322 Kilowatt hours (kWhs) of gas in each of the two monthly billing periods of summer

- up to 967 unused kWhs of gas which may be carried forward to the next billing period.

Finally, if you are paying for natural gas on any of the other Commitment Tariffs, the allowance in kWhs is as follows:

	Yearly Tariff	Two monthly allowance in summer	Two monthly allowance in winter	Max. no. of kWhs for carry forward
Double Up Discount	3,600	468	732	1,406
Economy	4,395	586	879	1,758
Super Saver	5,889	791	1,172	2,373

FREE BOTTLED GAS REFILL ALLOWANCE

If your home is not connected to an electricity/natural gas supply but you would otherwise satisfy the conditions of the Free Electricity/Natural Gas Allowance Scheme, you may qualify for a Free Bottled Gas Refill Allowance. If so, you will receive a book of vouchers covering the following periods:

Period	Amount
January to April	5 vouchers
May to June	2 vouchers
July to August	2 vouchers
September to December	5 vouchers

Each voucher can be exchanged for a cylinder of gas at a retail outlet of your choice. The allowance does not provide for the cost of buying or hiring empty cylinders or for the delivery of cylinders of gas.

FREE ELECTRICITY (GROUP ACCOUNT) ALLOWANCE

You may qualify for this allowance if you are living in self-contained accommodation, i.e. a flat or apartment and if:

• you have your own electricity slot meter

• there are a number of separate electricity meters operating from one ESB meter, and the registered consumer of electricity is a landlord

• there are no separate meters, but the registered consumer of electricity at your address is a landlord.

The allowance is paid by a book of monthly payable orders, which may be cashed at your local Post Office and used to pay your electricity costs.

FREE TELEPHONE RENTAL ALLOWANCE (FREE TO ALL PEOPLE AGED 75 AND OVER FROM OCTOBER 2000)

This allowance covers the normal two monthly rental charge on your telephone line as well as the rental on a standard telephone handset. It also covers the cost of the first twenty call units used by you in each two monthly billing period.

The allowance may also cover the rental charge on certain additional equipment including:

• a second telephone socket installed by Eircom in another part of your home. Check with Eircom regarding the installation charge. (This is a handy night-time security measure — e.g. a second telephone socket by your bedside in case of an emergency)

• a telephone specifically designed for those with hearing or vision impairment. In such cases you may, if required, exchange your existing telephone for a Clarity telephone from Eircom. This special telephone handset has adjustable incoming speech volume, large keypad buttons and a "phone-ringing" flashing light indicator

• a special wall mounted bell for phone ringing amplification.

The conditions for receiving the Free Telephone Rental Allowance are somewhat similar to those for the Free Electricity Allowance and its associated allowances. The allowance may only be awarded if the telephone is registered in your name. If you are aged 75 or over and do not live in a hospital or other institution, you will qualify for telephone rental allowance regardless of who resides with you or where you live. If you are between 66 and 75, you must live either entirely alone or only with certain other people, for example:

• a dependant under the age of 18 or under the age of 22 if in full-time education

• a qualified adult under the age of 66 who is disabled

• a qualified adult aged 66 or over, if either you or he/she is disabled

• another person who is getting one of a number of specified social welfare payments. In this case, either you or he/she must be disabled

• other disabled people

• a person providing you or another person living with you, with constant care and attention if you or that other person is disabled.

FUEL ALLOWANCE

This is an allowance of £5 per week which is payable as part of your pension over a 26 week period each year from mid-October to mid-April. For those who live in cities and towns where there is a ban on the sale of bituminous coal (Dublin, Cork, Limerick, Wexford, Dundalk, Drogheda and Arklow), the allowance is increased to £8 per week.

To qualify for this allowance, you must satisfy a number of conditions, including:

1. Living alone.

2. Living only with other qualified pensioners.

Since October 1999, entitlement to the Fuel Allowance has been extended to pensioners who have access to their own fuel supply, provided they meet the other qualifying conditions of the scheme.

MEDICAL CARD

You may qualify for a medical card from your local health board, depending on the amount of your income. Your social welfare pension is taken into account in deciding your entitlement. The weekly income guidelines for a medical card for the year 2000 are set out below (Gross income less PRSI deductions):

	Single person living alone	Single person living with family	Married couple
Under the age of 66	£ 93.50	£ 88.00	£135.00
Age 66–69	£101.50	£ 88.00	£151.00
Age 70–79	£135.00	£117.00	£202.00
Age 80 or over	£142.00	£122.00	£212.00

These guidelines may be increased in certain circumstances as indicated below:

	Per Week
For each child under the age of 16	£16.50
Other dependants	£18.00
House expenses e.g. rent, mortgage	£16.00
Cost of travelling to work	£14.50

If you do not satisfy these guidelines but have special needs, you may still qualify for a medical card.

DRUGS PAYMENT SCHEME

This is an important new scheme that covers families and individuals for the cost of their prescribed medication. Under the scheme, no individual or family will have to pay more than £42 in any calendar month for approved prescribed drugs, medicines and appliances for use by that person or his/her family in that month.

Family expenditure covers the nominated adult, his/her spouse (including a person with whom he/she is living as husband or wife) and children under 18 years. Dependants over 18 and under the age of 23 years who are in full-time education may also be included. A dependant with a physical disability or a mental handicap or illness who cannot maintain himself/herself fully, who is ordinarily resident in the family home and who does not hold a current medical card, may be included in the family expenditure under this scheme regardless of age.

It is important to complete a registration form (available from your health board) immediately to ensure that you/your family can avail of the new scheme, which commenced on 1 July 1999. Return the completed form to your health board.

SCHEME OF COMMUNITY SUPPORT FOR OLDER PEOPLE

This scheme is designed to support initiatives to improve the security and social support for vulnerable older people. Any voluntary or community based organisation working with or providing support for the elderly may apply for a grant under the scheme. Grants are available for small-scale physical security equipment such as:

• the strengthening of doors and windows

• window locks

* door chains and locks

* security lighting

* socially monitored alarm systems including the pendant or button alarm system which is operated via the telephone and is worn around the wrist or neck.

The scheme is aimed at people aged 65 years or over who are living alone or living in households made up exclusively of older people, or of older and other people who are dependent, vulnerable and unable to purchase or install the equipment themselves.

For enquiries about the Free Schemes, contact: 071 69800 (ext. 8371) or 01 8748444 (ext. 8371) or 01 7043371.

Customer Service
If you have any complaints to make in relation to the quality of service you receive from the Department of Social Welfare, please write to the Customer Service Manager, Pension Services Office, College Road, Sligo, or Tel. 071 69800 (ext. 7187).

REFERENCES

Department of Agriculture, Food and Forestry, "Scheme for Early Retirement from Farming", *Farming,* January 1994.

Department of Social, Community and Family Affairs Explanatory Booklets.

National Social Services Board, *Entitlements for the Over 60s,* published by NSSB-Dublin, September 1998.

Retirement Planning Council of Ireland, *The Retirement Book,* published by the Retirement Planning Council of Ireland, September 1998.

The Irish Family Handbook 1999.

The Law and Older People, published by the National Council on Ageing and Older People, Report No. 51, Dublin, 1998.

List of Social Welfare Information Leaflets and Booklets

SW10	Checklist for Pensioners
SW16	Old Age Non-Contributory Pension
SW17	National Fuel Scheme
SW19	Rates of Payment
SW39	Free Electricity/Gas Allowance and TV Licence
SW40	Free Travel
SW41	Carer's Allowance
SW45	Free Telephone Rental Allowance
SW47	Bereavement Grant
SW54	Supplementary Welfare Allowance
SW60	Pensioners and Savings
SW85a	Scheme of Community Support for Older People
SW99	Social Welfare and the Euro

MAXIMUM WEEKLY INCREASES FROM MAY 2000 — TABLES 1–3

Table 1
Increases in Maximum Weekly Rates of Social Insurance from May 2000

Personal and Qualified Adult Rates	Present Rate £	New Rate £
Retirement Pension/Old Age Contributory Pension:		
(i) Under 80		
Personal rate	89.00	96.00
Person with qualified adult under 66	144.50	156.20
Person with qualified adult aged 66 or over	148.90	160.60
(ii) 80 or over		
Personal rate	94.00	101.00
Person with qualified adult under 66	149.50	161.20
Person with qualified adult aged 66 or over	153.90	165.60
Widow's/Widower's Contributory Pension:		
(i) Under 66	77.10	81.10
(ii) 66 and under 80	82.10	89.10
(iii) 80 or over	87.10	94.10
Invalidity Pension:		
(i) Under 65		
Personal rate	75.20	79.20
Person with qualified adult under 66	124.70	132.50
Person with qualified adult aged 66 or over	124.70	137.20

Personal and Qualified Adult Rates	Present Rate £	New Rate £
(ii) 65 and under 80:		
Personal rate	89.00	96.00
Person with qualified adult under 66	138.50	149.30
Person with qualified adult aged 66 or over	138.50	154.00
(iii) 80 or over:		
Personal rate	94.00	101.00
Person with qualified adult under 66	143.50	154.30
Person with qualified adult aged 66 or over	143.50	159.00
Occupational Injuries Benefit —		
Death Benefit Pension:		
Personal rate	95.40	99.40
Occupational Injuries Benefit —		
Disablement Pension:		
Personal rate	97.20	101.20
Disability/Unemployment Benefit:		
Personal rate	73.50	77.50
Person with qualified adult	116.70	124.50
Injury Benefit/Health and Safety Benefit:		
Personal rate	73.50	77.50
Person with qualified adult	116.70	124.50
Orphan's Contributory Allowance:	51.60	55.60

Table 2
Increases in Maximum Weekly Rates of Social Assistance from May 2000

Personal and Qualified Adult Rates	Present Rate £	New Rate £
Old Age Non-Contributory Pension:		
(i) Under 80		
Personal rate	78.50	85.50
Person with qualified adult	122.70	137.20
(ii) 80 or over		
Personal rate	83.50	90.50
Person with qualified adult	127.70	142.20
Blind Person's Pension:		
(i) Under 66		
Personal rate	73.50	77.50
Person with qualified adult under 66	116.70	124.50
Person with qualified adult aged 66 and over	117.70	129.20
(ii) 66 and under 80:		
Personal rate	78.50	85.50
Person with qualified adult under 66	121.70	132.50
Person with qualified adult aged 66 and over	122.70	137.20

(iii) 80 or over:		
Personal rate	83.50	90.50
Person with qualified adult under 66	126.70	137.50
Person with qualified adult aged 66 and over	127.70	142.20
Widow's/Widower's Non-Contributory Pension:		
(i) Under 66	73.50	77.50
(ii) 66 and under 80	78.50	85.50
(iii) 80 and over	83.50	90.50
One-Parent Family Payment (including one child):		
(i) Under 66	88.70	92.70
(ii) 66 years and over	73.70	100.70
Carer's Allowance:		
(i) Under 66	76.50	80.50
(ii) 66 years and over	81.50	88.50
Disability Allowance:		
Personal rate	73.50	77.50
Person with qualified adult	116.70	124.50
Supplementary Welfare Allowance:		
Personal rate	72.00	76.00
Person with qualified adult	115.20	123.00
Unemployment Assistance (short-term):		
Personal rate	72.00	76.00
Person with qualified adult	115.20	123.00
Unemployment Assistance (long-term):		
Personal rate	73.50	77.50
Person with qualified adult	116.70	124.50
Pre-Retirement Allowance/Farm Assistance:		
Personal rate	73.50	77.50
Person with qualified adult	116.70	124.50
Orphan's Non-Contributory Pension:	51.60	55.60

Table 3
Increases in Maximum Weekly Rates of Health Allowances from May 2000

	Present Rate £	New Rate £	Present Rate Euro	New Rate Euro
Supplementary Allowance payable to Blind Persons in receipt of a Blind Pension				
(i) Blind Pensioner	22.80	24.00	28.95	30.47
(ii) Blind Married Couple	45.60	48.00	57.90	60.95
Infectious Diseases Maintenance Allowance				
(i) Personal rate	73.50	77.50	93.33	98.40
(ii) Persons with qualified adult	123.00	130.40	156.18	165.57

USEFUL ADDRESSES

Department of Social, Community and Family Affairs — Head Offices

Áras Mhic Dhiarmada
Store Street
Dublin 1
Tel. 01 874 8444
Disability Benefit Enquiries

- information service

- information on PRSI

- EU International Organisation Liaison Section

- voluntary and community services (704 3866 for Dublin callers)

- Supplementary Welfare Allowance (704 3866 for Dublin callers).

Townsend Street 1
57–164 Townsend Street
Dublin 2
Tel. 01 874 8444

- information on Unemployment Assistance or Benefit

- occupational injuries benefits.

Department of Social, Community and Family Affairs
PO Box 3840
Dublin 2
Tel. 01 704 3165 or 01 704 3867

- Employment Support Services

- Back to Work Allowance

- Employers' PRSI Exemption scheme.

Department of Social, Community and Family Affairs
PO Box 3988
Dublin 1
Tel. 01 704 3875/6

- summer jobs scheme for students.

Oisín House
212–213 Pearse Street
Dublin 2
Tel. 01 874 8444 and 01 704 3266

• accounts branch

• butter vouchers.

O'Connell Bridge House
Social Welfare Services Office
D'Olier Street
Dublin 2
Tel. 01 874 8444

• International Records

• PRSI (Refund of Contributions) Section (704 3266 for Dublin callers)

• EU Records.

Gandon House
Amiens Street
Dublin 1
Tel. 01 874 8444

• Central Records Office.

Marlborough Street
101–104 Marlborough Street
Dublin 1
Tel. 01 874 8444 and 01 704 3075

• Social Welfare Inspectors

• Scope Section (insurability of employment).

Letterkenny
Social Welfare Services Office
St Oliver Plunkett Road
Letterkenny
County Donegal
Tel. 074 25566 or 01 874 8444

• Child Benefit

• Treatment Benefits (Dental and Optical – 704 3925 for Dublin callers)

• Aural Benefits (704 3908 for Dublin callers)

Longford
Social Welfare Service Office
Government Buildings
Ballinalee Road
Longford
Tel. 043 45211 or 01 874 8444

- Pre-Retirement Allowance (704 3322 for Dublin callers)
- Disablement Benefit (704 3473 for Dublin callers)
- Carer's Allowance for carers of people getting Invalidity Pension or Disability Allowance (704 3331 for Dublin callers)
- Maternity Benefit (704 3475 for Dublin callers)
- Adoptive Benefit (704 3475 for Dublin callers)
- Health and Safety Benefit (704 3478 for Dublin callers)
- Death Benefit (704 3473 for Dublin callers)
- Family Income Supplement (FIS) (704 3322 for Dublin callers)
- Rent Assistance (PPO)
- Disability Benefit (PPO) (704 3473 for Dublin callers)
- Disability Allowance (704 3948 for Dublin callers)
- Invalidity Pension (704 3322 for Dublin callers)
- Bereavement Grant (01 704 3487 for Dublin callers).

Waterford
Department of Social, Community and Family Affairs Social Welfare Services Office
Cork Road
Waterford
Tel. 051 874177 or 01 874 8444

- Self-Employment Section
- special collection system for non-PAYE employees
- voluntary contributions.

Sligo
Pension Services Office
College Road
Sligo
Tel. 071 69800 or 01 874 8444

- Blind Person's Pension (704 3331 for Dublin callers)

- Old Age Pension (704 3331 for Dublin callers)
- Retirement Pension (704 3311 for Dublin callers)
- Deserted Wife's Benefit/Allowance
- Orphan's Allowance (704 3385 for Dublin callers)
- Prisoner's Wife's Allowance
- Widow's and Widower's Pensions (704 3385 for Dublin callers)
- One-Parent Family Payment
- Carer's Allowance (other than that previously mentioned)
- Free Bottled Gas Refill Allowance
- Free Telephone Rental Allowance
- Free Television Licence
- Free Travel.

Local Social Welfare Offices and Health Boards

See your telephone directory for details of your local Social Welfare Office — also listed in the Guide to Social Welfare Services SW4.

Enquiries regarding health services should be made to the appropriate health board. The health boards have local offices in the various counties covered by them.

Eastern Health Board
Dr Steeven's Hospital
Dublin 8
Tel. 01 679 0700 or Freephone 1800 520 520

North Eastern Health Board
Kells
County Meath
Tel. 046 40341

Southern Health Board
Wilton Road
Cork
Tel. 021 545011
Customer Information Helpline 1850 742000 (from Southern Health Board regions)

Mid-Western Health Board
31–33 Catherine Street
Limerick
Tel. 061 316655
Customer Service 061-483287

South Eastern Health Board
Lacken
Dublin Road
Kilkenny
Tel. 056 20400

North Western Health Board
Manorhamilton
County Leitrim
Tel. 072 20400

Western Health Board
Merlin Park Regional Hospital
Galway
Tel. 091 751131

Midland Health Board
Arden Road
Tullamore
County Offaly
Tel. 0506 21868

Chapter Six

Community and Residential Care

In 1996, it was estimated that the number of older people requiring at least a moderate level of care was 102,900, (i.e. approximately 25 per cent of the population over the age of 65). This is expected to increase to 176,000 by 2026 (an increase of 71 per cent).

COMMUNITY CARE SERVICES

Health boards and voluntary organisations provide various community care services.

Public Health Nursing

Public health nursing is a key service for maintaining the elderly and other groups in the community rather than placing them in residential care. However, the workload of community nurses is such that routine visiting of the elderly and other groups requiring long-term care is greatly restricted.

Community Social Workers

Community social workers also have a role regarding the care of the elderly in the community, but again, the resources currently available are limited.

Home Helps

Home helps provide assistance with home care and personal care tasks. Some health boards provide home helps directly, while others give grants to voluntary bodies to organise the service. There are currently almost 12,000 home helps involved in the health services, the majority of whom work part-time. The number of individuals who benefit from the home help service is currently around 20,000.

Meals on Wheels

Meals on wheels are provided almost entirely by voluntary groups that are grant aided by health boards.

Day Centres

Day centres help to ease the burden of caring for relatives while making a range of non-medical services available to their clients. There is no legal obligation on health boards to provide day centres. The majority of centres are operated by voluntary bodies with grants from health boards. It is estimated that at the end of 1996, there were 4,000 places available in day centres.

RESIDENTIAL CARE

Residential care consists of care in a geriatric hospital ward, a nursing home, retirement home or sheltered accommodation. Sheltered accommodation usually provides grouped housing with a range of support services, including a warden and/or an alarm system.

NURSING HOME OPTIONS

Voluntary Homes

These are individually run, mainly by religious groups or trusts. They have their own application forms and procedures. They receive some funding from the health board. You apply directly to the matron for a vacancy, but there is usually an extensive waiting list.

Private Homes

These can vary considerably in terms of the type of care provided. Very few homes specialise in caring for residents with specific problems, such as dementia, which requires full-time nursing care, while others will take only residents who are reasonably independent. Many homes cater for both categories of people.

Health Board Homes

Health boards provide institutional care for the elderly in a variety of settings, including geriatric hospitals and district hospitals. There is no direct charge for such care, but the hospital retains most of the elderly person's Old Age Pension as a contribution towards the cost of care. If an elderly person is in a private nursing home, the health board provides a subvention towards the nursing home's charges on a means test basis. The amount of the subvention varies from a minimum of £70 to a maximum of £120 per week. This depends on the person's level of dependency.

An elderly person can be accommodated in a health board public nursing home, but there is a huge shortage of places in these homes. Places are usually given to people in chronic situations with very little income who have been occupying beds in public hospitals but cannot be returned to the community.

Hospice Care

The hospice movement has a health care philosophy which aims to bring healing, love, empathy and caring to all patients. It can provide specialised palliative care, day care services and home care services to patients as well as occupational therapy where required.

If a person is in the fortunate financial position of being able to choose a particular nursing home, then there are a number of factors to consider.

CHOOSING A NURSING HOME

Regulations

First of all, it should be noted that under the Nursing Homes (Care and Welfare) Regulations 1993, the registered proprietor and the person in charge of a nursing home must have a brochure available with information about the nursing home. This should include the name and address of the home, the name of the registered proprietor, the admissions policy, the accommodation provided as well as special facilities and services.

Prepare Carefully

First of all, discuss all the options with your family. Make sure you have explored all the possibilities of using home and community based care, even on a private basis. Discuss the decision with your family doctor and public health nurse, and obtain a full medical assessment to ensure nursing home care is really required. Identify medical, physical and social needs, and whether or not the nursing home meets those needs in relation to the following:

- level of nursing care required
- continence care
- special dietary requirements
- pre-terminal or terminal care requirements
- management of essential medications
- extent of supervision required
- suitability for walking aid or wheelchair, if necessary.

If a nursing home is required specific points to consider are:

1. Is the atmosphere cheerful and friendly?
2. Are the staff helpful, friendly and informative?
3. Are nurses on duty around the clock or is there a 24-hour phone access?
4. Can your own GP visit the home?
5. Do the following services also operate from time to time and what are the charges, if any, for same:
   (a) laundry
   (b) hairdressing
   (c) arrangements for television, newspapers, books, etc.

In relation to the premises, it would be appropriate to obtain information on the following:

1. The number of beds in the home and whether the rooms are single or shared.
2. Is there a lift?
3. Are there en suite facilities?
4. Is there a choice of dining facilities?
5. Are there religious facilities?
6. Is there a garden/conservatory?
7. What occupational therapy is provided?
8. Can residents bring some of their own possessions into the home?

9.   Are family members encouraged to visit their relatives at all times?

Finally, anyone considering the option of living in a nursing home can contact an agency to discuss the particular nursing home that might be suitable. The agency will try and match the needs of the older person with the best nursing home available, as the agency will have all the relevant information concerning specific nursing homes in the area. (A list of such agencies is set out at the end of this chapter.)

THE REGULATION OF NURSING HOMES

The regulation of nursing homes and standards in relation to care and welfare in nursing homes are set out in the Health and Nursing Homes Act 1990 and regulations made under the Act. Under the Nursing Home (Care and Welfare) Regulations 1993, it is stated that the registered proprietor and the person in charge of a nursing home shall ensure that the following are provided for dependent persons maintained in a nursing home:

- suitable and sufficient care to maintain the person's welfare and well being, bearing in mind the nature and extent of the person's dependency

- a high standard of nursing care

- appropriate medical care by a medical practitioner of the person's choice or acceptable to the person

- facilities for the occupation and recreation of persons

- opportunities to participate in activities appropriate to his/her interests and capacities

- freedom to exercise choice to the extent that such freedom does not infringe on the rights of other persons

- privacy to the extent that the person is able to undertake personal activities in private

- information concerning current affairs, local matters, voluntary groups, community resources and events

- adequate arrangements to facilitate a person in the practice of his/her religion.

In addition, the registered proprietor and the individual in charge of the nursing home shall encourage dependent persons to maintain contact with persons of their choice and be allowed reasonable times for receiving visitors.

Health Board Inspections of Private Nursing Homes

Every six months, a medical director of the local health board is obliged to inspect private nursing homes.

The director prepares a report which outlines the standard of the medical care in the home, the correct staffing levels which should be maintained, the number of patients, the dependency level of the patients, the safety of the rooms, whether medical care is administered appropriately, the activities and occupational therapy provided for patients and on the nursing home facilities for enabling GPs to examine patients and prepare medical reports. However, at present, these reports do not cover details of complaints about the nursing home.

The Information Commissioner has recently (February 2000) directed that the public have a right to obtain copies of these reports of health board inspectors of private nursing homes.

Every three months, an Environmental Health Officer is also obliged to inspect nursing homes to ensure that the nursing homes comply with the hygiene regulations.

The Eastern Regional Health Authority

From 1 March 2000, the Eastern Regional Health Authority took over as the statutory body responsible for health and personal social services for the 1.3 million people who live in Dublin, Kildare and Wicklow. Three new area health boards, the Northern Area Health Board, the East Code Area Health Board and the South Western Area Health Board, have responsibility to deliver within their own areas, the services previously provided by the Eastern Health Board. The headquarters of the Eastern Regional Health Authority is Dr. Steeven's Hospital, Dublin 8 (Tel. 6790700).

CODE OF PRACTICE FOR NURSING HOMES

A code of practice for nursing homes was published by the Department of Health in July 1995. This has been agreed by a group of people representing proprietors of nursing homes, health boards, the National Council on Ageing and Older People, carers and other people with experience of caring for older people.

The purpose of the code is to set out the best standards of care to which all nursing homes should operate. It covers a range of issues, including the philosophy of care, the involvement of residents in decision making, legal and financial issues and the provision of services (including health services and medication).

While the code is not legally binding, it does set standards for high quality care and encourages nursing homes to achieve these standards.

The code of practice deals with a number of issues:

Philosophy of Care

A nursing home must endeavour to create an environment that seeks to develop, maintain and maximise the full potential of each resident. A resident should be treated with respect. Staff should be sensitive to their individual needs and abilities. The management of the home should be flexible and promote individual care.

Contracts of Care

Under Article 7 of the Nursing Homes (Care and Welfare) Regulations 1993, a written contract of care must be agreed between the registered proprietor, the prospective resident and/or the person responsible within two months of admission to a nursing home. The contract should cover:

- services to be provided for the resident
- the level of fees, time and method of payment, whether in advance or arrears
- extra services and appliances that are charged separately
- a procedure for increasing fees when this is necessary
- a provision for a review of placement
- the personal items the resident may bring to the home and those the home will be expected to provide
- the arrangement for the care of pets, where pets are allowed
- the terms under which the resident can vacate accommodation temporarily, whether for holidays or admission to a hospital
- the circumstances in which the resident might be asked to leave
- the statement of insurance cover of the home and the responsibility for insuring personal valuables
- a provision for the observance of the religious beliefs of the resident
- the procedure on the death of a resident, taking into account the known

wishes of the resident

• arrangements for holidays away from the home.

General Reviews

A comprehensive nursing review of each resident should be undertaken by the nursing home at least once every six months.

Health Services

Admission to a home should not diminish a person's access to the health and welfare services available in the community and in acute hospitals. This includes the right to choose a general practitioner, consultation in private at any time and consultation on the independent request of the general practitioner.

Domestic Routines

Domestic routines are necessary for the smooth running of the home. Nevertheless, they need to take into account both the needs and preferences of the individual together with the desirability of a lifestyle which is as normal as possible.

Involvement of Residents in Decision Making

With regard to the routines of a home, residents should be involved as much as possible in making decisions that affect them.

Modes of Address

The way elderly people are addressed and the use of names are important. It is important to take account of individual preference in the way names are used.

Medication

Each nursing home must have a written policy and procedures for nurses on the administration of medical preparations.

Restraint

Restraint is the use of physical or chemical means to control the movement of a resident. Restraint should only be used to prevent injury to the resident or to other residents.

Residents' Access to Personal Records

People have a right to know what is said about them in the records kept in relation to them. It is good practice for the staff of a nursing home to share information with residents in the context of an open and professional relationship. Residents who wish to have access to written records should be able to do so.

Privacy and Personal Autonomy

It is desirable that residents in long-term care should have their own room unless they prefer otherwise. They should also have access to communal areas. Spouses who wish to do so should be allowed to share a room.

Activities

Residents who are able to should be encouraged to pursue existing interests or acquire new ones and to help around the home, provided that such activities do not interfere unduly with others.

Residents' Property

Taking possessions into the nursing home can help people maintain lifelong interests and can also help create a more homely atmosphere. The number and type of possessions that residents can take with them to the home will depend on the policy of the home.

Financial Affairs

People planning to move to a nursing home should be tactfully encouraged by their relatives or friends to make a will. Nursing home staff should be able to advise those who have not made a will, or the relatives of the person moving to the home, where they may obtain independent advice. Residents or other relatives should not be referred to the registered proprietor's own solicitor. Registered proprietors or staff should not, except in exceptional circumstances, act as witnesses to any patient's will. In *no* circumstances should the registered proprietor or any member of the staff become an executor of a resident's will.

Complaints

There should be a procedure within the nursing home to deal with in-house complaints, without prejudice to the formal complaints procedure provided in the Nursing Homes (Care and Welfare) Regulations.

Special Needs of the Terminally Ill

Staff of nursing homes should be aware of the special needs of the dying and of the particular skills required in nursing a dying patient.

NURSING HOME SUBVENTIONS

Applications for a subvention must be made to the local health board by or on behalf of a person before his/her admission to a nursing home. To qualify for a subvention, one must be sufficiently dependent to require maintenance in a nursing home and unable to pay any or part of the cost of the maintenance in the home.

Assessment of dependency is carried out on behalf of the health board by a doctor, nurse, occupational therapist or physiotherapist. The assessment includes an interview with the person and his/her nearest relatives, if any. It must include an evaluation of the ability of the person to carry out the tasks of daily living as well as the level of social support available to that person.

For the purposes of a nursing home subvention, the means test evaluates the income of the applicant and the inputed value of his/her assets together with the income and value of the assets of a spouse.

A health board may refuse to pay any subvention if the applicant's assets, excluding the principal residence, exceed £20,000 or if the principal residence is valued at £75,000 or more. The application may also be refused if the residence is not occupied by a spouse, a child aged under 21 or in full-time education, a relative in receipt of a disability allowance and certain other disability benefits, or if the applicant's income is greater than £5,000 per annum.

The rules also stipulate that the value of any property not exempt from the means test is taken into consideration for means testing and that 5 per cent of the property's value is considered to be an annual income. For example, if a person entering a nursing home owns a property or assets worth £100,000 and applies for a subvention, he/she is considered to have an additional income of £5,000.

How much is the subvention? There are three maximum weekly rates of subvention which a health board may pay. These are:

1. £120 per week (maximum dependency).

2. £95 per week (high dependency).

3. £70 per week (medium dependency).

These relate to the degree of nursing care you require as assessed by the officer of the health board.

FINANCING LONG-TERM RESIDENTIAL CARE

All payments by an individual to an approved nursing home where that individual is residing can be fully set off against that person's income for tax purposes.

Covenants

Covenants are dealt with in more detail in Chapter 3. However, a child or other relation could provide a deed of covenant for an older person to assist with nursing home fees. The donor can then claim income tax relief on payments made under the deed of covenant. (Note: there is no gift or inheritance tax payable when a person receives benefits to cover the cost of a nursing home where the beneficiary is permanently residing and the beneficiary cannot care for himself/herself because of physical or mental infirmity.)

Payments Direct to Nursing Home for Dependent Relatives

This relief is granted if you or your spouse have a relation (which includes either parent) who is a dependent relative, i.e. one who is incapacitated or if not incapacitated, is the widowed mother or mother-in-law of the tax-payer and the dependent relative is in receipt of a State Old Age Pension with a total income below £5,152 (for the year ended 5 April 2000). In these circumstances, you or your spouse are able to claim the Dependent Relative's Allowance (DRA) of £110 for income tax purposes. By claiming the DRA, you or your spouse can also claim tax relief on any contribution either of you make to the relative's medical expenses, including the cost of maintenance in a recognised nursing home or hospital. There is no need to execute a Deed of Covenant to claim tax relief where this situation applies. The income threshold for this relief for the year ended 5 April 2001 will be about £5,500.

Equity Release Plans

Many older people are "asset rich" but "income poor", i.e. their incomes are low but they may have considerable liquid assets, often tied up in their home, to which they cannot gain access. A number of equity release plans have been launched in recent years in the UK, which vary in degrees of success. To date, no similar products have emerged in Ireland, but it would be possible for such a scheme to be arranged privately between an older person and a relation or friend, provided both parties received independent legal advice. Examples of these equity release plans are outlined below:

Mortgage annuities: with a mortgage annuity, the capital raised by securing a mortgage on a property is used to purchase an annuity in the insurance market. The balance of the annuity, after the cost of servicing the mortgage, is available as a contribution to long-term care costs or for general living expenses. If the annuitant dies before the mortgage term has expired, the balance of the outstanding loan is a first charge on the sale of the property.

Home reversion: under basic home reversion plans, a portion (or all) of the property is purchased by the investor who then leases it back, rent-free, to the existing occupant. The house reverses back to the investor when specified events happen, such as a death (of the last survivor in the case of married couples), moving away permanently (typically into residential long-term care) or the sale of the property. If only part of the property is involved in the reversion, the individuals share proportionally in any increase in the value of the property when it is sold.

Health insurance to cover long-term nursing home care: VHI and BUPA do not provide any nursing home cover in Ireland except for convalescing after an operation. In the UK, BUPA offers cover for long-term nursing home care that begins at 65 years of age. In 1998 this involved a monthly payment of £90 for men and £115 for women (due to a longer life span). In addition, BUPA also offers a benefit of £1,000 per month. Norwich Union offers similar policies but there are no plans to introduce them to Ireland.

LIST OF AGENCIES THAT ASSIST WITH QUERIES RELATING TO NURSING HOMES OR CARERS

1. Retirement Association of Home Information Service Ltd.
    158 Stillorgan Road
    Donnybrook
    Dublin 4
    Tel. 01 269 1832
    Contact: Ann O'Dwyer.

2. Sharing the Caring
    4 Leopardstown Grove
    Blackrock
    County Dublin
    Tel. 01 278 0801

3. David Vinten operates a nursing home helpline: Tel. 1560 22 23 24

4. Care for the Elderly at Home Ltd.
    14 South Leinster Street
    Dublin 2
    Tel. 01 662 3423

5. Irish Registered Nursing Homes Association
    c/o Lakeland Mount Pleasant
    Loughrea
    County Galway
    Tel./Fax. 091 755018

6. Private Home Care
    Professional Care Consultants
    14 The Village Centre
    Lucan
    County Dublin
    Tel. 01 624 5369 or 01 288 0000

A list of nursing homes can be obtained from individual health boards.

Chapter Seven

Savings and Investments

INTRODUCTION TO INVESTMENTS

People who are fortunate enough to have funds to invest either before retirement age or during retirement need to examine a number of issues before deciding what investment decision to make. Such issues include:

- the income requirements of the individual concerned

- what percentage of the savings can be invested purely for capital growth

- the length of time the investment period should last, i.e. a number of months or a number of years

- whether the investments should be low risk, medium risk or high risk

- whether it is possible to realise the funds at short notice and the potential penalties that might arise in the absence of notice

- the tax liabilities that may arise with the savings.

The following list contains some of the options available for investors:

1. Deposit accounts with banks, building societies and credit unions. The rates can vary greatly depending on the institution, the amount invested and whether the monies are on demand, deposit or fixed term deposit.

2. Post office schemes, such as savings bonds and savings certificates, are all tax-free returns and provide a regular income if required.

3. Stock Exchange investments.

4. Investment funds where investors pool their resources to create a common investment fund that is controlled by professional managers. These funds can provide greater security, as the risk is spread over a diverse range of investments. However, the investments can range from a very high risk to a medium risk to a very low risk.

5. Investments under certain tax incentive schemes such as the business

expansion scheme, film industry investments, forestry funds and certain property investment schemes.

Deposit Accounts

The rate of return on deposit accounts is very low, so even a large lump sum will provide a rather small income. It is important to ascertain the rates at a number of different financial institutions. Alternatively, an investment consultant could assist. One such firm is National Deposit Brokers Ltd. These consultants operate a software system called Rateline, which tracks all the interest rates and financial packages on offer and assesses which gives the best return. They can advise a client what the best rate is, depending on what the person wants from the investment. The client is not charged for this advice because the company receives a fee from the financial institution when a deposit is made. It is also possible to get a copy of their report, *Investing for Income* by phoning 1800 322 422. This outlines the best options for the small investor. Nevertheless, current deposit rates after DIRT tax hardly compensate the saver for effective inflation. The address of National Deposit Brokers Ltd is The Old Distillery Building, Beresford Street, Dublin 7 (Tel: 01 8724000).

DIRT Tax

A DIRT tax of 24 per cent is payable on ordinary deposit accounts and a DIRT tax of 20 per cent is paid on special savings accounts. DIRT tax on deposit interest will be reduced to 22 per cent from 6 April 2000 (Budget 1999).

Special Savings Accounts (SSA)

The following conditions apply to special savings accounts:

• the investor must live in Ireland

• £75,000 is the maximum anyone can hold (£150,000 per couple)

• there can only be one account per person

• no withdrawals can be allowed within the first three months of the account being opened

• 30 days notice of withdrawal is required

• two years is the maximum time for an account.

These accounts are subject to DIRT tax at 20 per cent. Some financial institutions offer slightly higher rates on SSAs, which makes them a more attractive option.

Credit Unions

Every pound you invest with the credit union is converted into a single share, and dividends or interests are paid on the shares at the end of each year. The dividend can vary between credit unions but has averaged at about 5 per cent in recent years. If you own shares in a credit union there is a free life savings insurance scheme which matches the value of your shares up to a maximum of £10,000 in the event of your death if you are under the age of 55. If you are over 55 when you die, the following are the additional amounts paid by the credit union to your estate:

1.   If you are between 55 and 59: 75p for every share.

2.   If you are between 60 and 64: 50p for every share.

3.   If you are between 65 and 70: 75p extra for every share.

Reclaiming DIRT Tax

If you are not liable for income tax and you are either over 65 years of age or permanently incapacitated, then you are entitled to claim back any DIRT tax deducted from deposit interest you have earned. In the case of a married couple, it is sufficient for either partner to be over 65 years of age.

Post Office Schemes

An Post offers investment opportunities (which are all tax-free) and include:

• normal savings banks where funds can be placed on deposit

• instalment savings

• savings certificates

• savings bonds.

Web Site

An Post has a web site at www.postoffice.ie

An Post Deposit Accounts

An Post has a number of deposit accounts on offer, such as an instant access deposit account in which interest is calculated daily and added to your account from 31 December each year. In addition, there are fixed term accounts, which require that you leave your money with them for an agreed period of time, usually from one to twelve months. The interest can be higher than interest paid by other banks.

National Instalment Savings

This saving facility is open to anyone who is at least seven years of age and who makes regular monthly payments between £20 and £300 for at least one year. During the first twelve months of contributions, no interest is paid. The annual returns are:

• after year 1: 2 per cent

• after year 2: 2 per cent

• after year 3: 2.5 per cent

• after year 4: 3.2 per cent

• after year 5: 4.5 per cent.

Savings Bonds

These are a three year investment and require a minimum investment of £100. The rate of return (from 23 December 1998) is 8 per cent tax-free over a three year period, which is equivalent to an average annual rate of return of 2.6 per cent if held for the full term. Individuals may invest up to £60,000. Joint holdings are subject to a maximum of £120,000. No interest is paid on money withdrawn during the first year.

Savings Certificates

These are another tax-efficient way to save your money at no risk. The current issue (sixteenth issue, effective from 23 December 1998) is offering a tax-free return of 16 per cent interest, guaranteed and tax-free over a five and a half year period. This is the equivalent of an average annual tax-free rate of 2.74 per cent per annum if the investment is held for the full term. An individual can hold up to £60,000 worth of savings certificates or £120,000 for a married couple. Savings certificates can pay a regular half-yearly income. Since the rate of interest is lowest in the early years and highest in the later years, you should try to avoid withdrawing money towards the end of the five year period, when the returns are greatest.

PURCHASING STOCKS AND SHARES ON THE STOCK EXCHANGE

Irish Government Stocks/Bonds

Government stocks/bonds, or gilts as they are sometimes called, could be an attractive investment for the ordinary investor. One of their attractions is that no DIRT tax is deducted from the interest. The advantage of government stocks is that there is a fixed rate of interest or dividend paid each year until the stock is redeemed, after a few years. This is unlike dividends or shares, which can fluctuate depending on the profits of the companies concerned from year to year. The National Treasury Management Agency (NTMA) has recently issued stocks close to prevailing interest rates. Interest on these bonds is liable to income tax. They can be purchased below their redemption value, providing a tax-free capital gain when they are redeemed.

Equity Investments

Investments in shares (commonly referred to as equities) are designed to provide both capital and income growth over a term normally in excess of five years. As such, investments do not have a capital guarantee and the funds invested are at risk of a loss as well as a gain. A way to manage this risk is to diversify investment exposure over a spread of companies in different industry sectors and geographical regions. In a favourable economic environment, the dividends paid by companies tend to increase well above the rate of inflation.

Goodbody Stockbrokers have quoted the following performances for a lump sum of £1,000 invested for the five years up to 1998:

1. Cash: £1,324.

2. Government bonds: £1,555.

3. Property: £2,715.

4. Irish shares: £3,055.

Anyone considering an investment in shares should be aware that share prices can fall as well as rise. General advice given to potential investors is that they should never invest money in shares if they cannot afford to lose some or all of that money, especially if the investment is in more volatile areas, such as oil exploration or high-tech companies.

Buying shares does not carry any tax implications, but selling may. Selling shares could give rise to capital gains tax (CGT) if you make a profit on the sale. Your liability to CGT is calculated by taking a cost of the shares, applying a revenue index based on the year of purchase to allow for inflation, and subtracting this from the proceeds received from the sale of the shares. This is the amount of your capital gain. There is an annual CGT exemption of £1,000 for a single person and £2,000 for a married couple.

INVESTMENT FUNDS

These are pooled investments, where each individual investor's money is pooled with that of other investors. The whole fund is managed on their behalf by professional managers. These funds can provide greater security for smaller sums invested as the risk is spread. Outlined below are some examples of investment funds:

Managed Funds

If you are prepared to take a risk with your capital, then a managed fund may be an option. By choosing this route, you can opt for various levels of risk. These involve a secure fund geared towards steady capital growth, a medium risk balanced fund or a higher risk, more specialised fund. The advantage of a managed fund is that a pooled investment, liable for 22 per cent withholding tax at source, gives you access to a wider range of stocks than you might be able to reach by going directly to the Stock Market.

Some managed funds give a guarantee that your capital will be returned in full after a period of five years if the investment did not increase in value.

PIPS and PEPS

Personal Equity Plan (PEP): PEPS are funds invested entirely in equities (shares) usually with a sufficient proportion in Irish shares to qualify for a lower rate of tax (20 per cent).

Personal Investment Plan (PIP): PIPS are invested in managed unit funds with a reasonably broad mix of Government unit bonds, shares and cash. They carry no upfront charges but you will pay an annual management charge of around 1.75 per cent. The minimum contributions are approximately £40 to £50 per month for the PIP and £100 for the PEP. PIPS are taxed at 24 per cent and PEPS at 20 per cent. Usually an investment of five years or more is recommended. PIPS and PEPS give access to the markets for relatively small investors through managed funds.

Property Funds

For investors who are nervous of shares, one alternative could be to buy into property funds, which are invested in commercial property. Although these funds do not provide capital guarantees, they are generally considered low to medium risk investments. Property has proved a strong performer in Ireland. Between 1970 and 1997 for example, property was the top performing asset class in nine different years, according to Bank of Ireland Asset Management. It was beaten only by equities (shares), which performed best on twelve occasions, cash, which enjoyed four years of supremacy and bonds, which finished top on three occasions. However, such funds can become quite illiquid during a downturn in the property market, so investors may not be able to realise their funds in such circumstances.

Tracker Bonds

Tracker bonds are usually set up as either deposits or life assurance policies. Trackers provide a return based on the growth in a Stock Market index or basket of Stock Market indices.

Tracker bonds are another possibility for those who want to participate in Stock Market gains while protecting at least a portion of their initial investment. Part of your investment (usually a minimum of £5,000) is placed on deposit or invested in income bonds to cover the capital guarantee. The remainder is used to buy an option in selected Stock Market indices (such as the FTSE 100, the Nikkei 225, and so on). Most offer a guarantee that the investor will at least get his or her money back at the end of the agreed period. Some offer a minimum return on top of that basic guarantee. The maximum return possible is usually based on the performance of a Stock Exchange index or a mix of indices. For instance, the return may be linked to the performance of the FTSE 100 index of British Stock Market prices. The net proceeds of the investment are tax free, as all relevant taxes are paid directly by the insurance company.

Bank of Ireland Asset Management has also produced a booklet for starter investors entitled *Guide to the Stock Market*. The guide shows what you can expect from four different types of investment — deposit, property, bonds and shares — over varying periods from 5 to 30 years. It measures how a sample investment of £10,000 in each category performed in these periods and calculates which gave the best overall return.

With Profit Bonds

These invest in the same type of assets as other pooled investments. Nevertheless, the investment is normally for ten years or more. There is a guaranteed sum assured at the end of the term. A bonus is added each year to the guaranteed sum and a bonus may be added at the end of the term. The investment may also incorporate a life policy that is guaranteed to pay a sum assured if you die, but will pay out the cash value of the accumulated annual premiums or a guaranteed sum if you cancel/encash the policy after a number of years.

Guaranteed Income Bonds

Under this investment a lump sum is invested for a fixed term, usually three, four or five years. At the end of the term the original investment is returned. During the term you can receive a guaranteed tax paid income on a monthly, quarterly, half-yearly or yearly basis. However, you cannot withdraw during the fixed term without incurring penalties and these are highest in the early years of the bond. In deciding whether or not to invest in a guaranteed income bond, see how they compare with the prevailing bank rate.

Guaranteed Growth Bonds

Guaranteed growth bonds are similar to income bonds except that the interest accumulated is paid out to you at the end of the term together with the original investment. The returns are paid to the investor after the fund has already paid tax. It is possible to cash in your bond before the end of the term but the amount payable may be less. It is important to hold the bond for the term selected. In the event of your death your original investment, together with your accrued interest, is paid out to your estate.

Mutual Funds

Unit Trusts: these are probably the simplest way of investing in stock markets and involve a group of investors, a fund manager who manages the investment and a trustee who supervises the fund manager and makes sure that the job is done properly.

Unit-Linked Bonds: a unit-linked bond is very similar to a unit trust. The difference is that the unit based fund has a life assurance policy attached to it and does not have trustees. Unit-linked bonds, offered by most insurance companies, give you access to a wide range of investment opportunities and expertise. A unit-linked bond is an open-ended investment, which you can cash in at any stage. It can be set up to provide you with a regular income, or alternatively, you can take partial encashments as required. There are up to 100 different bonds to choose from. These fall into a number of different categories:

1.   Property bond: invests in shops, offices, factories.

2.   Equity bonds: invests in company shares.

3.   Fixed interest (gilt): invests in government securities.

4.   Cash bond: invests in cash deposit and short-term gilts.

5.   International equity bond: invests in company shares abroad.

6.   Managed bond: this is the most popular of unit-linked bonds and employs a mix of the other sectors.

Your lump sum is used to buy units in one or more of a range of investment bonds. When choosing particular bonds it is wise to spread the risk. For example, the return on most unit-linked bonds is not guaranteed. It could be spectacular or it could be poor, and it depends on the performance of the particular bond selected. Also, the initial charge has to be recouped before the bond begins to make a profit. For these reasons you should consider this type of investment only in the long-term, as a five to seven year investment at minimum. Should you wish to cash in your investment in whole or in part within the first few years you may lose out because the set-up, administration and commission charges are up to 5 per cent.

The main advantages of unit-linked bonds are the fact that all returns have tax paid and that in the medium to long-term they will probably provide a return comfortably in excess of inflation. Also, unit funds may offer an element of capital growth, which many investors look for. A disadvantage is the absence of a guaranteed rate of return, as unit prices can fall as well as rise.

INVESTMENTS UNDER CERTAIN TAX INCENTIVE SCHEMES

Business Expansion Scheme

Designed to help smaller companies raise venture capital, these schemes are usually promoted in the weeks leading up to the end of the April tax year and provide tax relief at the maximum rate on sums invested up to a maximum of £25,000 (a married couple can get an allowance of £50,000 on the condition that they both have an income of £25,000 in their own right). This is considered a relatively high-risk investment option. You must also leave your funds untouched for at least five years.

Section 35/Film Industry Investment

These investments are high risk but with at the maximum rate for every pound invested. The tax relief is available on 80 per cent of your investment (up to a maximum of £25,000 per annum) but you can realise your investment after just one year (presuming there is a fund left and any profits). This relief has been extended in the 1999 Budget until the 5 April 2005.

Forestry Funds

In an effort to encourage farmers and other landowners to convert land to forestry, substantial tax relief is available for investment in forestry schemes, either going into the investment or with profits being distributed tax-free at maturity.

SUMMARY

In short, cash is the most secure form of investment, but it gives the lowest return. The one consistent advice all consultants give their clients is to *spread the risk*.

Chapter Eight

Income Tax and Capital Gains Tax

INTRODUCTION

Retired people are subject to taxation in almost exactly the same way as everyone else. Nearly all income (including social welfare and occupational pensions) is liable to tax. However, extra tax-free allowances are available to older people. While it is true that many retired people do not have to pay any tax, this is because their income is below the tax exemption level. It does not mean that they are not liable for tax.

Residents

Income tax is payable in Ireland if the individual is resident in the country in any given tax year, and is subject to exemptions for foreign source income and to any double treaties that may apply. Non-Irish residents are liable for income tax on Irish source income only. The rules about residents in relation to tax purposes are complex.

RSI Number

The Revenue and Social Insurance (RSI) number is the number each person must use when dealing with income and other taxes. It is the same number that is used for claiming social welfare payments. In the past, wives had the same tax number as their husbands and this continues to be the case for many older people.

Married Couples

A married couple would be taxed in one of three ways:

1. They may be taxed jointly, which is what the tax authorities will do unless the couple chooses one of the other options. Most older couples are taxed in this way.

2. They may be taxed jointly, but have the tax-free allowances divided between them. This is usually called "separate assessment".

3.   They may each be taxed as a single person.

Unmarried Couples

Unmarried couples who live together are taxed as single people. They cannot opt for any other tax treatment.

Note: The following pages set out the position relating to Income Tax provisions, rates, bands, tables and personal allowances for the year ending 5 April 2000. The appendix at the end of this chapter sets out the changes for the tax year commencing on 6 April 2000, as announced in the Budget statement of the Minister for Finance on 1 December 1999.

INCOME TAX

Pay As You Earn

The vast majority of income tax is paid under the "pay as you earn" scheme (PAYE). The PAYE system aims to spread your tax liability as evenly as possible over the year. This would be relatively easy if there was only one rate of income tax, as the same rate would be applied throughout the year. However, you may pay income tax at two different rates depending on your level of income. For the tax year 1999/2000 (i.e. for the year ending 5 April 2000), the rates of income tax and the income levels to which they apply, are:

• for a single or widowed person: £14,000 at 24 per cent and the balance at 46 per cent

• for a married couple (jointly assessed): £28,000 at 24 per cent and the balance at 46 per cent.

Standard Rating of Personal Allowances

The tax year which started on 6 April 1999 introduced major changes in the way tax is assessed. Tax credits have been introduced from the beginning of the tax year 1999/2000. It is intended that tax credits will replace tax-free allowances entirely, but this will be done in stages. At present, some allowances, notably mortgage interest allowances and health insurance allowances, are granted at the standard rate of tax, i.e. at 24 per cent. From 6 April 1999, the single and married person's allowance of £4,200 and £8,400 respectively is only allowed at 24 per cent also.

Low Income Exemption Limits

People with limits below certain exemption limits are taken out of the income tax net altogether, although they would otherwise be liable for some tax if the calculations were done in the normal way. (See Chart 1 for exemption limits.)

ALLOWANCES

Tax-Free Allowance

This is the amount of income that everyone is entitled to get tax-free. There are three rates — married, single and widowed. The married allowance is given to couples who are jointly assessed for tax. There are a number of options available to married couples in relation to dividing the allowances between them. The tax situation of married, separated or divorced couples is complex and people should contact their local Inspector of Taxes for more information in this area, if required. The Widowed Person's Allowance is available to all widowed people. Widows or widowers who have dependent children may also be able to claim the One-Parent Allowance.

PAYE Allowance

This is a special allowance of £1,000 for people who pay tax through the PAYE system. The allowance is only allowed at the standard rate. This allowance is granted to all people liable to be taxed under the PAYE system. If a husband and wife are both earning wages, there is a double allowance of £2,000. It is allowed to a child working full-time in a family firm, but not to a spouse.

Age Allowance

If the taxpayer or his/her spouse is over or will reach the age of 65 during the tax year, extra allowances apply, all at the top marginal rate:

1. Single person: £400.

2. Widowed person: £400.

3. Married couple: £800.

Incapacitated Child Allowance

There is an allowance of £800 in respect of an incapacitated child, although this is reduced if the amount spent in maintaining the child is actually less. The child must have become incapacitated before reaching 21 years of age or while still receiving full-time education. There is no tax relief with regard to other children. Tax exemption limits are increased depending on the number of children in a family.

Dependent Relative's Allowance

This allowance of £110 is granted for each relative of the taxpayer or spouse who is incapacitated, and even if not incapacitated, where the relative is the widowed mother or mother-in-law of the taxpayer as well. The allowance is also granted in respect of a son or daughter of the taxpayer who is resident with them and on whose services he or his wife depend because of old age or illness.

One-Parent Family Tax Allowance

A one-parent family allowance is an allowance you may claim if you are a single parent (whether widowed, single, deserted, separated or divorced) and you have a child who is dependent on you. The one-parent family allowance, where due, is given in addition to your normal personal allowance. To obtain the allowance, the single parent must not be living with another person.

A single parent with a dependent child or children can claim this allowance (a couple living together as man and wife may not claim). A child includes, in addition to a child of your own, a stepchild, a formally or informally adopted child and any child of whom you have custody and control and who you maintain at your own expense. Such a child is regarded as a dependant of yours if he/she is:

- born during the tax year or is under sixteen years of age at the beginning of the tax year

- is over sixteen years and receiving full-time education or undergoing a training course for a trade or profession for a minimum of two years

- is over sixteen years and permanently incapacitated, either physically or mentally, from maintaining himself or herself and had become so before reaching 21 years of age or finishing full-time education.

The child must live with the claimant for the whole or part of the year of claim.

If the child has income in his/her own right, the income may be reduced by the amount that income exceeds £720.

There are two different amounts of this allowance — widowed people may get a One-Parent Allowance of £3,700 in 1999/2000 and other lone parents may get an allowance of £4,200. This allowance is partially standard rated for the year 1999/2000. (See Chart 1.)

Blind Person's Allowance

An allowance of £1,500 is available to a single blind person and £3,000 to a blind couple in 1999/2000. It will continue to be treated in the normal way as an allowance.

Bereavement Allowance

There are special extra allowances for widowed parents with dependent children in the five years following the death of their spouse. (There are also special arrangements for tax in the year of death — these depend on the tax arrangements of the couple prior to the death and apply whether or not there are dependent children.) The bereavement allowances are in addition to the widowed person and one-parent family allowances. (See Chart 1 for details.)

Tax Allowance to Employ a Carer

In general, until 1999/2000 there were no tax-free allowances available if you employed someone in your home to look after the family, do the housework or mind the children. However, there has been an allowance if you or your spouse is totally incapacitated and you employ a person to look after the incapacitated person. This allowance will now be available if the person employed looks after any family member who is incapacitated. This includes a relation of the marriage or if you are a legal guardian of an incapacitated person. There is a special form for claiming this allowance. The amount of the allowance is £8,500 or the cost of paying the carer, whichever is less. It will be treated in the normal way in 1999/2000.

Allowances

Home Carer's Allowance

The Finance Bill 2000 provides for a new tax credit of £3,000 for families where one spouse works at home to care for children, the aged and incapacitated persons. This credit will be granted at the standard rate of income tax and was introduced as a balancing measure to the controversial "individualisation" proposals of the Budget. The stay-at-home spouse will be allowed to earn up to £4,000. If the income of the spouse exceeds this limit (not taking into account income from a Carer's Allowance from the Department of Social, Community and Family Affairs), marginal relief is available. In this circumstance, the £3,000 credit is reduced by £3 for every £1 of income over £4,000. See table below.

Earnings	Additional Carer's Credit
£4,000	£3,000
£4,100	£2,700
£4,200	£2,400
£4,500	£1,500
£4,800	£ 600
£4,900	£ 300
£5,000	Nil

The £3,000 credit will continue to be available for the first year in which the claimant enters or re-enters employment outside the home where income for such employment substantially exceeds £4,000. As a result, the time of re-entry into employment might need to be considered.

Health Insurance

If you pay premiums to an authorised insurer, you may get tax relief in the following year. Virtually all other expenditure reliefs apply in the year in which the expenditure is incurred. This relief is already standard rated. You get relief at the standard rate in 1999/2000 for the full amount of premiums being paid in 1998/1999.

Permanent Health Benefit

If you pay premiums under a permanent health benefit scheme approved by the Revenue Commissioners, which provides periodic payments to an individual in the event of loss or reduction of income due to ill health, the amount of the premium on which you get tax relief is limited to 10 per cent of your income. This relief will be treated in the normal way in 1999/2000.

Health Expenses

Every individual is entitled to claim relief for specified health expenses incurred during the tax year if those expenses are not otherwise recoverable under a contract of insurance or by compensation. Allowances in relation to health expenses may be claimed personally in respect of dependent family members. Health expenses are defined as involving:

• the services of a practitioner (including a nurse)

• diagnostic procedures carried out on the advice of a practitioner

• maintenance of treatment in a hospital

• drugs or medicines supplied on prescription (which are not recovered by the Health Board or under Contract of Insurance)

• supply, maintenance or repair of any medical, surgical, dental or nursing appliance used on the advice of a practitioner

• physiotherapy or similar treatment prescribed by a practitioner

• orthoptic (eye treatment) or similar treatment prescribed by a practitioner

• transport by ambulance

• hearing aids

• wheelchairs/wheelchair lifts.

Only health expenses incurred in the provision of health care are eligible for relief. Health care is defined as meaning the "prevention, diagnosis, alleviation or treatment of an ailment, injury, infirmity, defect or other disability".

The definition of health care specifically excludes routine opthalmic or dental care. Maintenance or treatment in a hospital includes maintenance or treatment in a nursing home. Maintenance paid to a nursing home for a dependent relative for whom the taxpayer receives a Dependent Relative Allowance can qualify for income tax relief.

There is no upper limit to the amount of deductible health care expenses. However, the first £100 for one person, or £200 for a family, does not qualify. The allowance may be claimed either in the year in which the expense was incurred or the year in which it was paid. You must make a separate claim for these expenses at the end of the tax year — a special form (Med. 1) is available from the Inspector of Taxes. Among the items which may be claimed are nursing home bills.

Pension Contributions

If you are contributing to an approved personal pension scheme, your contributions are deducted from your pay before tax is assessed. From 6 April 1999, the maximum amounts in which relief on premiums are paid to secure a retirement annuity will be as follows:

1. Under 30 years of age: 15 per cent of net relevant earnings.

2. 30–39 years of age: 20 per cent of net relevant earnings.

3. 40–49 years of age: 25 per cent of net relevant earnings.

4. 50 years of age and over: 30 per cent of net relevant earnings.

The 30 per cent limit will also apply to persons of any age in certain defined occupations with a limited earning span, e.g. sports athletes, entertainers.

Private Rented Accommodation

People paying rent for the private rented accommodation in which they live are eligible for tax relief. The maximum amount of the relief is age related:

• under 55 (single person): £500 (£750 for 2000/01)

• over 55 (single person): £1,000 (£2,000 for 2000/01)

• widowed person under 55: £750 (£1,125 for 2000/01)

• widowed person over 55: £1,500 (£3,000 for 2000/01)

• under 55 married couple: £1,000 (£1,500 for 2000/01)

• over 55 married couple: £2,000 (£4,000 for 2000/01).

Landlords are obliged to maintain records for the purposes of this relief. The relief is available for rent paid in the current year and continues to be treated in the normal way. For those under 55, the tax relief is at the standard rate and for those over 55 it is at the marginal rate. Under the Finance Bill 2000 the rent itself is only allowed at 22 per cent (the standard rate of tax for 2000/01).

Mortgage Interest

Mortgage interest relief has been granted at the standard rate for some years. The maximum amount of interest paid which attracts relief is:

- single person: £2,500

- married couple: £5,000

- widowed person: £3,600.

You may claim 80 per cent of the mortgage interest paid, subject to these limits — the maximum interest relief for a married couple is £3,800 (80 per cent of £5,000). The first £100 of mortgage interest paid by single and widowed people and the first £200 paid by a couple does not get tax relief. There are special arrangements for new mortgage holders. New mortgage holders can get 100 per cent interest relief up to the limits mentioned above for the first five years (the £100/£200 deduction does not apply either). The tax relief allowed is only at the standard rate of tax. Under the Finance Bill 2000 the relief allowed at the standard rate of tax for 2000/01 is £4,000 for married or widowed persons and £2,000 for single persons. The same relief applies for new mortgage holders.

The only interest on which you may get tax relief is in borrowings to buy, repair/improve your principal private residence or to buy/improve the main residence of a former or separated spouse or a dependent relative (one for whom you can claim the Dependent Relative Allowance). If you take out a second mortgage on your house, the interest payable will only attract tax relief if you can show that the money was used to repair/improve the house. Thus, if you remortgaged to pay for education or other expenses you will not get tax relief on the interest paid.

If you have to take out a bridging loan while selling one house and buying another, you may also claim tax relief on that loan, up to the same maximum amount as outlined above (this is in addition to your normal entitlement). Interest paid on other personal loans does not attract tax relief.

Tax Relief for Service Charges

Income tax relief at the standard rate of 24 per cent is available for 1999/2000 if you paid service charges in full and on time for 1998/1999 with the maximum qualifying for the relief being £150. Alternatively, if a son or daughter who lives with you pays the service charges they may claim the relief. (See the Revenue information booklet, *Tax Relief for Service Charges IT27,* for details.)

LUMP SUM PAYMENTS ON REDUNDANCY/RETIREMENT

Generally speaking, all payments made by employers to employees and directors are regarded as "pay" for tax purposes. Employers must operate PAYE on such payments unless they are exempt from tax or the tax office gives other instructions.

Lump sum payments on a redundancy or retirement, however, qualify for special tax treatment — they may be exempt from tax or may qualify for some relief in tax.

The redundancy or retirement lump sum is exempt from tax if it is a statutory redundancy payment (this is an individual statutory entitlement under employment legislation), or if the employment consisted of foreign service and certain other conditions are met.

The following redundancy and retirement payments, although not exempt from tax, qualify for some relief from tax. These are:

- salary or wages in lieu of notice on redundancy or retirement

- non-statutory redundancy payment, i.e. the amount payable by your employer which is over and above the statutory redundancy payment. The non-statutory redundancy payment is also known as a "golden handshake" or an "*ex gratia* payment", e.g. a person gets a lump sum of £20,000 which includes statutory redundancy of £5,000. Up to £15,000 is taken into account and the £5,000 is ignored for tax purposes.

What Tax Relief Is Available?

On your first redundancy or retirement payment, the higher of the following will be exempt from tax:

(a) basic exemption

(b) increased exemption

(c) standard capital superannuation benefit (SCSB).

(a) Basic Exemption

The basic exemption from 1 December 1998, is £8,000 plus £600 for each full year of service with the employer making the redundancy payment. For example, Mary gets a lump sum of £10,000 when she leaves her employment after ten and a half years service. The basic exemption due to her is £14,000, i.e. (£8,000 + £600 x 10). There is, therefore, no tax due on the lump sum of £10,000 as it is under £14,000 — the basic exemption in

Mary's case.

(b) Increased Exemption

If you are not a member of an Occupational Pension (Superannuation) Scheme or if you irrevocably give up your right to receive a lump sum from the pension scheme, the basic exemption as outlined above can be increased by £4,000. The basic exemption is therefore increased to £8,000 + £4,000 + £600 for each full year of service.

If you are in an Occupational Pension Scheme, this increased exemption of £4,000 is reduced by the amount of any tax-free lump sum from the pension scheme to which you may be immediately entitled, or the present day value at the date of leaving employment of any tax-free lump sum which you may be able to receive from the pension scheme in the future.

If the lump sum from the pension scheme is more than £4,000, you are not due the increased exemption. If it is less than £4,000, you are due the increased exemption of £4,000 less the amount of the pension scheme entitlement.

(c) Standard Capital Superannuation Benefit (SCSB)

This benefit is calculated by the formula:

$$A + N/15 = L$$

Where A = one year's average of the remuneration for the last three years of service; B = the number of complete years of service; and L = any tax-free lump sum received or receivable under an approved superannuation scheme.

REFUND OF DEPOSIT INTEREST RETENTION TAX

If you or your spouse are over 65 years of age or either of you are permanently incapacitated, your income (including deposit interest) for the year 1999/2000 must be equal to or below the following limits:

	Single/Widowed Person	Married Couple
Up to the age of 65:	£4,100	£ 8,200
Age 65 and over:	£6,500	£13,000

If your income is below the above limits, then you are entitled to a full refund of tax paid on deposit interest, including deposit interest on special savings accounts.

The income limits above are increased for those who have dependent children, by £450 for each of the first two and by £650 for each subsequent child.

If you do not already make a tax return, you can get a claim form 54D from your nearest tax office.

If you have applied for a refund in previous tax years, your tax office will automatically send you the form 54D to enable you to claim any refund that may be due. If you already make a tax return, you can make your claim by completing your annual tax return.

You will find the address and telephone number of your nearest tax office in the telephone directory. If you live in Dublin, Meath, Kildare or Wicklow you can telephone 01 874 6821, ext. 2256 for information or write to the Inspector of Taxes (Claims Section, Findlater House, 28/32 Upper O'Connell Street, Dublin 1).

HOW TO COMPLAIN TO THE REVENUE

If you have a complaint to make to the Revenue Commissioners, there are a number of procedures to follow.

In the first instance, the complaint should be brought to the attention of the Revenue staff in the office concerned, either orally or in writing. The staff there will try to resolve your complaint without delay.

If your complaint cannot be resolved by the Revenue staff, or if you are unhappy with the response to it, you can ask for the complaint to be reconsidered by the local manager. Local managers are responsible for all issues concerning their office and should be able to investigate and resolve your complaint.

In the event that you are still unhappy with the response, you should contact the Customer Service Policy Unit, which will arrange for your complaint to be investigated. The unit can be contacted by telephone or in writing at the Office of the Revenue Commissioners, Customer Service Policy Unit, Corporate Management Division, Castle House, South Great George's Street, Dublin 2 (Tel. 01 679 2777).

CAPITAL GAINS TAX

Capital Gains Tax (CGT) is a tax on gains realised when an asset is disposed of and a gain to the owner arises. It was first introduced in 1974.

Persons Chargeable

All persons resident in the State for tax purposes are liable to CGT. Individuals who are resident and domiciled in Ireland are chargeable on all gains wherever arising.

Assets

All forms of property, wherever located, are assets for the purposes of CGT. Assets include goodwill in a property or an option, any interest in property (e.g. a lease) and it also includes debts and foreign currencies, except those specifically exempted.

Disposal

Disposal of an asset includes any transfer of ownership of the asset by way of sale, exchange, gift or transfer to the trustees of a settlement. CGT can also arise on a part disposal, i.e. where less than the whole of an asset is disposed of. If someone inherits an asset in the case of a death, no chargeable disposal takes place and the person who receives the asset is treated as acquiring it at the market value at the date of death.

Computation of Gain

A chargeable gain accruing on a disposal of an asset is calculated by deducting the cost of the acquisition of the asset and any expenditure incurred on its enhancement, such as improvements made to a property by an extension, from the consideration received, e.g. money paid over for the disposal.

Indexation Relief

When you sell an asset, the original cost and enhancement expenditure may be increased by indexation before any CGT liability is calculated. If an asset is acquired prior to 6 April 1974, the "cost" to be indexed is the market value as of 6 April 1974 rather than the original cost.

Indexation relief does not apply to development land. The table of inflation/indexation multipliers is set out at the end of this chapter.

Married Couples

Transfers between spouses do not give rise to a CGT charge — the spouse who received the assets is deemed to have acquired it on the date and at the cost at which the other spouse acquired it.

Capital Gains Tax Rates

From 3 December 1997, a single rate of 20 per cent applies to most chargeable gains. Prior to this the rate was 40 per cent. Development land gains are chargeable at 40 per cent. Nevertheless, the 20 per cent rate will apply to the disposal of development land between 23 April 1998 and 5 April 2002, provided the land has outline planning permission at the time of disposal. After 5 April 2002, the CGT on development land will be increased to 60 per cent.

From 1 December 1999, the 20 per cent rate of CGT will also apply to the disposal of non-residential development land and the disposal of residential development land to connected persons (as defined) (announced in Finance Bill 2000).

Exemptions and Reliefs — Annual Allowance

On 6 April 1998, the first £1,000 of chargeable gains for an individual in each tax year is exempt. This is an individual allowance and is not transferable between spouses.

Principal Private Residence

No CGT arises on the disposal of your main residence and grounds of up to one acre, provided it has been occupied by you throughout the entire period of ownership.

Gain on the Sale of a Residence

Up to an acre of land that has been provided for the sole occupation of a dependent relative as his/her sole residence is also exempt from CGT. A "dependent relative" in this regard includes any relative who, because of incapacity or infirmity, is not able to maintain himself or herself. Also included is the widowed mother of either spouse, who need not be incapacitated.

Tangible Moveable Assets

A gain arising to an individual on such assets is exempt if the total consideration received does not exceed £2,000.

Life Assurance Policies/Deferred Annuities

Disposals of these contracts are exempt from CGT in the hands of the original beneficial owner. A chargeable gain can arise on the disposal of such contracts by a person who is not the original beneficial owner if they acquire them for a consideration of money or money's worth.

Further Exemptions from CGT

Further exemptions from CGT include the following:

- bonuses on post office or State savings schemes
- gains on the disposal of government stocks
- gains on assets with a predictable life of under 50 years, e.g. a car, livestock, etc.
- winnings from lotteries, betting, etc.

Retirement Relief

When an individual aged over 55, who has owned a farm or business for more than ten years, disposes of that farm or business for a consideration of less than £250,000, the disposal is ignored for CGT. When the proceeds exceed £250,000, the CGT arising is restricted to the lower of half the difference between the proceeds and £250,000, or the CGT as computed in the normal way.

From 1 December 1999, the £250,000 threshold is increased to £375,000 (Finance Bill 2000).

Complete exemptions can be claimed by the individual meeting the above conditions if they give their farm/business to their child (or nephew/ niece working in the business). However, this exemption is lost if the recipient disposes of the farm/business within six years.

Rollover Relief

Under this relief, a person can defer the payment of CGT arising on the disposal of certain assets used solely for business purposes if the proceeds arising are reinvested in similar assets and used solely for business purposes. The assets which qualify for this relief are plant and machinery, land, buildings, goodwill and in certain circumstances, shares in private companies.

Death

If a person dies and the executors/administrators or beneficiary sell an asset which belonged to the deceased, CGT is based on the difference between the value of the asset on the date of death and the amount realised on the sale.

Computations of Gains and Losses

A Capital Gain is calculated by deducting the cost of the disposed asset from the proceeds of sale received when the asset is sold. If the asset is sold, more than twelve months after it was acquired, the cost of the asset is increased by inflation relief or indexation relief, i.e. where the cost is increased by the annual consumer price index for each year the asset is held before it is sold. The gain is calculated by multiplying the cost of the asset by the index factor relative to the tax year in which the purchase took place. The CGT and indexation factors are displayed at the end of this chapter.

Example: Computation of Liability on Sale of Investment Property

In May 1999, a married couple sold a house for £200,000. The costs of the sale amounted to £8,000. They had bought the house in August 1973 for £9,500. The market value of the house on 6 April 1974 was £10,000. The couple had added an extension costing £50,000 to the house in March 1990. The house was not the principal private residence and it was not development land. The couple had no other chargeable gains in the tax year 1999/2000.

Computation:

1. Sale price: £200,000 less expenses of sale of £8,000.

2. Net sale price: £192,000.

3. Deduct value on 6 April 1974 adjusted for inflation, i.e. £10,000 x 6.313 = £63,130. Also add 1990 expenditure adjusted for inflation, i.e. £50,000 x 1.261 = £63,050.

4. Total deductable amount is £126,180, i.e. £63,130 plus £63,050.

5. £126,180 from £192,000 = £65,820 = Taxable Gain.

6. Net Gain: £63,820 (i.e. £65,820 less married couple exemption of £2,000).

7. Tax at 20 per cent = £12,764.

Payment of CGT:

CGT is determined on a self assessment basis. An individual must calculate the tax due and make payment by 1 November in the year after the disposal was made. If a person disposes of an asset during the 1999/2000 tax year which is liable to CGT, the tax is due for payment on 1 November 2000. The 1999/2000 tax return must be filed by 31 January to avoid interest or penalty payments.

FURTHER INFORMATION

If any individual needs further information or assistance, he/she can telephone or write to his/her tax office. The address and telephone number is shown on your TFA Certificate. If you live in the Dublin area, you may call to any of the information offices:

1. Level 2, The Square, Tallaght, Dublin 24.

2. Cathedral Street, off O'Connell Street, Dublin 1.

3. 85/93, Lower Mount Street, Dublin 2.

Further information is also available from the Revenue Internet Site at: http://www.revenue.ie

REFERENCES

The Law and Older People (A Handbook for Service Providers — National Council on Ageing and Older People)
The Tab Guide 1999–2000.
February 1999 edition of Relate (National Social Services Board).
Revenue Leaflet Form IT5 on Refund of Deposit Interest Retention Tax.
Revenue Leaflet on 1999 Budget Summary.
Revenue Leaflet CS3 — *How to Complain to Revenue.*
Revenue Leaflet IT21 — *Lump Sum Payment Sum on Redundancies/Retirement.*
Revenue Leaflet IT4 — *Understanding PAYE Tax Tables.*
Revenue Leaflet IT9 — *One-Parent Family Allowance.*
Revenue Leaflet entitled, *1999 PAYE Information.*
Revenue Form CGT1 — *Guide to Capital Gains Tax.*
December 1999 Issue of Revenue Tax Briefing.

TABLE OF MULTIPLIERS FOR DISPOSAL

Year Expenditure Incurred	Multiplier for disposal in year ended 5th April									
	1991	**1992**	**1993**	**1994**	**1995**	**1996**	**1997**	**1998**	**1999**	**2000**
1974/75	5.221	5.355	5.552	5.656	5.754	5.899	6.017	6.112	6.215	6.313
1975/76	4.217	4.326	4.484	4.568	4.647	4.764	4.860	4.936	5.020	5.099
1976/77	3.633	3.726	3.863	3.935	4.003	4.104	4.187	4.253	4.325	4.393
1977/78	3.114	3.194	3.312	3.373	3.432	3.518	3.589	3.646	3.707	3.766
1978/79	2.877	2.951	3.059	3.117	3.171	3.250	3.316	3.368	3.425	3.479
1979/80	2.596	2.663	2.760	2.812	2.861	2.933	2.992	3.039	3.090	3.139
1980/81	2.247	2.305	2.390	2.434	2.477	2.539	2.590	2.631	2.675	2.718
1981/82	1.857	1.905	1.975	2.012	2.047	2.099	2.141	2.174	2.211	2.246
1982/83	1.563	1.603	1.662	1.693	1.722	1.765	1.801	1.829	1.860	1.890
1983/84	1.390	1.425	1.478	1.505	1.531	1.570	1.601	1.627	1.654	1.680
1984/85	1.261	1.294	1.341	1.366	1.390	1.425	1.454	1.477	1.502	1.525
1985/86	1.188	1.218	1.263	1.287	1.309	1.342	1.369	1.390	1.414	1.436
1986/87	1.136	1.165	1.208	1.230	1.252	1.283	1.309	1.330	1.352	1.373
1987/88	1.098	1.126	1.168	1.190	1.210	1.241	1.266	1.285	1.307	1.328
1988/89	1.077	1.105	1.146	1.167	1.187	1.217	1.242	1.261	1.282	1.303
1989/90	1.043	1.070	1.109	1.130	1.149	1.178	1.202	1.221	1.241	1.261
1990/91	—	1.026	1.064	1.084	1.102	1.130	1.153	1.171	1.191	1.210
1991/92	—	—	1.037	1.056	1.075	1.102	1.124	1.142	1.161	1.179
1992/93	—	—	—	1.019	1.037	1.063	1.084	1.101	1.120	1.138
1993/94	—	—	—	—	1.018	1.043	1.064	1.081	1.099	1.117
1994/95	—	—	—	—	—	1.026	1.046	1.063	1.081	1.098
1995/96	—	—	—	—	—	—	1.021	1.037	1.054	1.071
1996/97	—	—	—	—	—	—	—	1.016	1.033	1.050
1997/98	—	—	—	—	—	—	—	—	1.017	1.033
1998/99	—	—	—	—	—	—	—	—	—	1.016

TAX OFFICES

Any telephone enquiries can be made to your own tax office. Telephone enquiries of a general nature should be made to the local tax office if phoning from outside Dublin or to the Central Telephone Information Office (Tel. 878 0000) if phoning from the 01 area. Telephone 01 8780 100 to request tax and revenue forms and leaflets available 24 hours a day, 7 days a week.

Provincial Tax Offices — Addresses and Telephone Numbers

Athlone Tax District
Government Offices
Pearse Street
Athlone
County Westmeath
Tel. 0902 92681

Castlebar Tax District
Michael Davitt House
Castlebar
County Mayo
Tel. 094 21344

Cork Tax District
Government Buildings
Sullivans Quay
Cork
Tel. 021 966077

Dundalk Tax District
Earl House
Earl Street
Dundalk
Co. Louth
Tel. 042 932251

Galway Tax District
Hibernian House
Eyre Square
Galway
Tel. 091 563041

Kilkenny Tax District
Government Buildings
Hebron Road
Kilkenny
Tel. 056 52222

Letterkenny Tax Dist.
Government Offices
High Road
Letterkenny
County Donegal
Tel. 074 21299

Limerick Tax District
River House
Charlotte Quay
Limerick
Tel. 061 318711

Sligo Tax District
Government Offices
Cranmore Road
Sligo
Tel. 071 60322

Thurles Tax District
Strandhover
Thurles
County Tipperary
Tel. 0504 21544

Tralee Tax District
Government Offices
Spa Road
Tralee
County Kerry
Tel. 066 7121844

Waterford Tax District
Government Buildings
The Glen
Waterford
Tel. 051 873565

Wexford Tax District
Government Buildings
Anne Street
Wexford
Tel. 053 45555

Dublin Tax Offices
Addresses and Telephone
Numbers:

Dublin Tax (Income Tax)
District

1A Lower Grand Canal
Street
Dublin 2
Tel. 01 661 6444
(Self-Employed; Individuals/ Trusts)

Dublin Tax (Corporation
Tax) District
Lansdowne House
Lansdowne Road
Dublin 4
Tel. 01 668 9400
(Companies)

Hawkins House
Hawkins Street
Dublin 2
Tel. 01 677 5004
(VAT)

Dublin PAYE No. 1 and
PAYE No. 4
Arus Brugha
9/15 Upper O'Connell Street
Dublin 1
Tel. 01 874 6821
(Employees)

Dublin PAYE No. 2 and
PAYE No. 3
85/93 Lower Mount Street
Dublin 2
Tel. 01 661 6444
(Employees)

Claims Section
Findlater House
28/32 Upper O'Connell
Street
Dublin 1
Tel. 01 874 6821
(Refund of DIRT tax)

CHART 1

Summary of Tax Allowances, Rates & Exemptions

INCOME TAX ALLOWANCES

The following allowances, reliefs and rate bands apply for years ended 5 April 1999 and 5 April 2000

	98/99	99/00
	£	£
Personal Allowance		
Single Person	3,150	*4,200
Married Person	6,300	*8,400
Widowed Person at standard rate*	-	*4,200
Widowed Person at marginal rate**	3,650	500
Widowed Person (in year of bereavement)	6,300	*8,400
One-Parent Family		
Widowed Person (except in year of bereavement)		
at standard rate*	-	*1,050
at marginal rate**	2,650	2,650
Other Person (deserted, separated or unmarried)		
at standard rate*	-	*1,050
at marginal rate**	3,150	3,150
Child's Income Limit	720	720
Widowed Parent Allowance		
Bereaved in 1998/1999	-	5,000
Bereaved in 1997/1998	5,000	4,000
Bereaved in 1996/1997	4,000	3,000
Bereaved in 1995/1996	3,000	2,000
Bereaved in 1994/1995	2,000	1,000
Bereaved in 1993/1994	1,000	-
PAYE Allowance	800	*1,000
Age Allowance		
Single/Widowed	400	400
Married	800	800
Incapacitated Child Allowance Max	800	800
Child's Income Limit	2,100	2,100
Dependent Relative Allowance Max	110	110
Relative's Income Limit	4,848	5,152
Blind Allowance	1,000	1,500
Blind Allowance (both spouses blind)	2,000	3,000
Additional Allowance for a Guide Dog	650	650
Incapacitated Person - Allowance for Employing a Carer Max	8,500	8,500
Revenue Job Assist Year 1 (plus £1,000 per child)	3,000	3,000
Year 2 (plus £668 per child)	2,000	2,000
Year 3 (plus £334 per child)	1,000	1,000
Rent Allowance for under 55's (max.)		
Single	500*	500*
Widowed	750*	750*
Married	1,000*	1,000*
Rent Allowance for 55 and over (max.)		
Single	1,000	1,000
Widowed	1,500	1,500
Married	2,000	2,000
Mortgage Interest (max.)		
First Mortgage		
Single	2,500*	2,500*
Widowed	3,600*	3,600*
Married	5,000*	5,000*
Others		
Single	1,900*	1,900*
Widowed	2,780*	2,780*
Married	3,800*	3,800*

*   Relief is available at the standard rate of 24% only
**   Marginal rate is an individual's highest tax rate
    i.e. 24% or 46% as appropriate

Pension Contributions

From 6 April 1999, for self-employed individuals, proprietary directors or employees who are not in an occupational pension scheme, the maximum amount of pension contributions which will qualify for tax relief are as follows:

Age	% of Net Relevant Earnings
Under 30 years of age	15%
30 to 39 years of age	20%
40 to 49 years of age	25%
50 years of age and over	30%

The 30% limit also applies to persons whose income comes wholly or mainly from specified sporting activities.

Exemption Limits

	98/99	99/00
	£	£
Single/Widowed		
under 65	4,100	4,100
65 - 74	5,000	6,500
75 upwards	5,500	6,500
Married		
under 65	8,200	8,200
65 - 74	10,000	13,000
75 upwards	11,000	13,000

Additional for Dependent Children		
1st and 2nd child (each)	450	450
Each subsequent child	650	650
Marginal Relief Tax Rate	40%	40%

1 DECEMBER 1999 BUDGET CHANGES

(This extract is taken from the December 1999 issue of Revenue Tax Briefing)

Income Tax: Personal Allowances

In his Budget statement on 1 December 1999, the Minister for Finance announced the extension of the standard rating of personal allowances to cater for the introduction of a full tax credit system from 6 April 2001. A full list of the personal allowances which will be standard rated from 6 April 2000 is given in the chart below. Standard rating means that tax relief will be given at the standard rate of tax of 22 per cent.

Personal Allowance	1999/2000		2000/2001
	Amount at		
	Standard Rate 24%	Individual's Highest Tax Rate 24% or 46%	Amount at Standard Rate 22%
Single Person	£4,200	—	**£4,700**
Married Person	£8,400	—	**£9,400**
Widowed Person			
– without dependent children	£4,200	£500	**£5,700**
– with dependent children	£4,200	£500	**£4,700**
One-Parent Family			
Widowed Person	£1,050	£2,650	**£4,700**
Other Person	£1,050	£3,150	**£4,700**
Widowed Parent Allowance			
Bereaved in 1999/2000		—	**£10,000**
1998/99		£5,000	**£8,000**
1997/98		£4,000	**£6,000**
1996/97		£3,000	**£4,000**
1995/96		£2,000	**£2,000**
1994/95		£1,000	—
PAYE Allowance	£1,000	—	**£1,000**
Age Allowance			
Single/Widowed	—	£400	**£800**
Married	—	£800	**£1,600**
Blind Allowance			
One Spouse Blind	—	£1,500	**£3,000**
Both Spouses Blind	—	£3,000	**£6,000**
Incapacitated Child	—	Max. £800	**Max. £1,600**
Dependent Relative	—	Max. £110	**Max. £220**

Revenue: Tax Rates, Bands and Tables (from 6 April 2000)

The tax rates are being reduced by 2 per cent, from 24 per cent to 22 per cent and from 46 per cent to 44 per cent.

As part of a move towards the individualisation of the standard rate bands:

* the standard rate band will be widened from £14,000 to £17,000 for a single or widowed person without dependent children
* a new standard rate band of £20,150 will be introduced for a single or widowed person with dependent children
* the standard rate band for a married couple with one income will remain unchanged at £28,000
* the standard rate band for a married couple, both with income, will be £28,000 subject to an increase of up to £6,000. The increase will be the lower of £6,000 or the amount of the income of the spouse with the lower income — this increase is not transferable between spouses.

Tax Tables, Table Allowances and Tax Bands for 2000/2001 are:

Tax Table	Table Allowance	Bands of Taxable Income
	Single/Widowed without dependent Children	
A	Nil	£17,000 @ 22%
		Balance @ 44%
	Single/Widowed with dependent Children	
	Nil	£20,150 @ 22%
		Balance @ 44%
	Single/Widowed without dependent Children	
B	£8,500	All @ 44%
	Single/Widowed with dependent Children	
	£10,075	All @ 44%
	Married	
R	Nil	£28,000 (with increase of max. £6,000 — see above) @ 22%
		Balance @ 44%
S	£14,000 (with increase of max. £3,000*)	All @ 44%
	Marginal Relief Cases	
Z	Nil	All @ 44%

*The increase of up to £3,000 for Table S is not transferable between spouses.

Exemption Limits

Single/Widowed	1999/2000	2000/2001
General Limit (under 65 years of age)	£4,100	£4,100
65 years of age and over	£6,500	£7,500
Married		
General Limit (under 65 years of age)	£8,200	£8,200
65 years of age and over	£13,000	£15,000

Marginal Relief will continue to apply where income does not greatly exceed the relevant exemption limit.

The above exemption limits are increased by £450 for each of the first two dependent children and £650 for the third and subsequent child.

Rent Relief for Rented Accommodation

Rent relief will be increased as follows and will be available at the standard rate of 22 per cent.

Rent Allowance	Single	Widowed	Married
Under 55 max.	£750	£1,125	£1,500
Over 55 max.	£2,000	£3,000	£4,000

Mortgage Interest Relief

Home Loan Interest paid is allowable at the standard rate of 22 per cent and is subject to the following maximum amounts:

First Time Buyer (First Five years)
Single   £2,500
Married/Widowed   £5,000*

Others
Single   £2,000
Married/Widowed   £4,000*

The existing 80 per cent and £100/£200 (single/married, respectively) restrictions have been abolished.

*Widowed Person's limit is now the same as that of a married couple.

Taxation of Unemployment Benefit

Systematic short-time workers will continue to be exempt from tax on Unemployment Benefit in 2000/2001.

Benefit-in-Kind-Preferential Loans

The "specified" rate for the purposes of calculating the benefit-in-kind on preferential home loans is being reduced from 6 April 2000. The specified rates will be:

1. Home Loans: 4 per cent (previously 6 per cent).
2. Other Loans: 10 per cent (unchanged).

Chapter Nine

Separation and Divorce

INTRODUCTION

Sadly, marital breakdown can arise for couples of any age. Provisional Irish Labour Force Survey figures for November 1996, suggested that 85,600 were involved in broken marriages in the Republic of Ireland at that time. Approximately 8,000 divorce applications have been made between 27 February 1997, when divorce was introduced, and February 2000.

Counselling

If a solicitor is consulted by someone seeking a separation or divorce, the solicitor is obliged to discuss with the client the option of reconciliation using the services of a counsellor. The aim of marriage guidance counselling is to help a couple to resolve the marital difficulties in order to enable them to continue to live together as a married couple.

Mediation

If counselling is not a practical option, the solicitor is also obliged to discuss the possibility of mediation with the client. The aim of mediation is not to save the marriage or attempt to resolve the difficulties being experienced by the couple, but rather to try and agree on the terms on which the couple will separate and live apart. The solicitor is obliged to give the client a list of qualified mediators. Communications between spouses and their counsellors and/or mediators are not admissible as evidence in court. This allows couples to speak openly and without fear that matters stated in counselling or mediation will be used as evidence in court at a later stage.

If proceedings are commenced at any stage in the future for judicial separation or divorce, then the solicitors acting for the respective clients must certify that they have discussed the options of reconciliation and mediation with their client.

SEPARATION AGREEMENTS

If a couple wants to separate formally, the least expensive and most digni-fied way of finalising a separation is by both parties voluntarily entering into a deed of separation. Separation agreements are written contracts entered into between a married couple that set out the agreed terms on which the couple will separate. Separation agreements must be drawn up voluntarily and it is advisable that both parties receive separate and inde-pendent legal advice before signing such an agreement.

The main matters dealt with in a separation agreement are:

- agreement to live separately

- a non-molestation clause

- arrangements regarding children to include custody, access, holidays, etc.

- future ownership of property and other assets

- maintenance payments and lump sum payments

- indemnity from the debts of the other spouse

- succession rights

- pension provisions.

In many Deeds of Separation, the parties usually state that they intend the agreement to be in full and final settlement of any possible future claims of either party. This is inserted to prevent the terms of the separation agree-ment being varied at a later stage. However, this clause is not legally bind-ing, but may carry weight with a court. In subsequent court proceedings, the court can vary the terms of the separation agreement which contains this clause, if it decides that it is appropriate to do so.

Outlined below are points to be noted relating to separation agree-ments:

- the law does not permit a spouse to contract out of future maintenance payments in a separation agreement

- if one spouse is making a claim in relation to another spouse's pension or life assurance policies, it may be necessary to apply to the court for a judicial separation, as the trustees of a pension scheme or a life assur-ance company may not be bound by an agreement concluded between two spouses unless the agreement is also made a formal order of the court.

JUDICIAL SEPARATION

If the couple cannot agree on a legal separation and cannot or do not wish to apply for a divorce, then a judicial separation can be applied for.

Under Section 31(4) of the Judicial Separation and Family Law Reform Act 1989, the jurisdiction to hear proceedings for a judicial separation may only be exercised "while either of the spouses is domiciled in the State on the date of the application commencing proceedings or is ordinarily resident in the State throughout the period of one year ending on that date".

The 1989 Act allows a decree of judicial separation on any one (or more) of six grounds:

1. Adultery.

2. Unreasonable behaviour.

3. One year's continuous desertion.

4. One year's separation (with consent).

5. Three year's separation (without consent).

6. No normal marital relationship for at least one year (this is the usual ground in most cases).

The document issued to begin judicial separation proceedings in the Circuit Family Court is called a Family Law Civil Bill. The High Court also has the jurisdiction to hear these proceedings but most cases are heard in the Circuit Court, where legal fees will be lower.

Once the judicial separation proceedings have been issued and before the court fully hears the case, a spouse may seek preliminary orders to ensure proper financial provision for himself/herself and the children before the hearing of the action.

Before the judicial separation is heard, spouses may also seek a barring order preventing the other spouse from entering the family home, a custody (or access) order in relation to any dependent children and orders for the protection of the family home, furniture and personal belongings.

On the granting of, or following a decree of judicial separation, the Circuit Court or High Court can make a number of orders relating to maintenance or specific assets. These orders are known as ancillary orders.

Under a judicial separation, either spouse, or in some cases a person acting on behalf of a dependent child, can apply to the courts to have one or more ancillary orders made in relation to maintenance, the family home, property, pension benefits, life assurance policies and succession rights.

DIVORCE

Divorce was introduced by the Family Law (Divorce) Act 1996. This came into force on 27 February 1997. Once divorce is granted, both parties are free to remarry subject to giving three months notice under the Family Law Act 1985. For avoidance of doubt, it is also stated that the divorce does not affect the rights of parents to be joint guardians of their infant children.

A divorce may be granted only when four conditions are all fulfilled:

1. The spouses have lived apart for at least four of the previous five years before proceedings began.

2. There is no reasonable prospect of a reconciliation between the spouses.

3. Both spouses, and any dependent children, have been (or will be) properly provided for.

4. Either spouse was domiciled in the State when proceedings began (or lived in the State for at least one year before that date).

Courts to Re-Examine All Issues on Application for Divorce

Under the Divorce Act 1996, the courts have to ensure that all issues such as maintenance, custody, access, etc. have been satisfactorily resolved in the interests of the spouses and in particular the interests of the children of the marriage. This means that if separation agreements have been entered into many years before an application for divorce is made, the court may very well deem it essential to consider in detail the provisions of the agreement and if necessary, alter these provisions.

If the spouses have lived apart for a period of at least four years, either spouse may apply for a divorce. Therefore, a spouse who is at fault or who has caused the breakdown of the marriage by for example, desertion, can apply for a decree of divorce after a period of four years has expired.

Orders can be made in the following areas relating to judicial separation or divorce proceedings:

• arrangements regarding children

• maintenance

• the family home

- other assets
- pensions and life policies
- domestic violence
- death and inheritance.

ORDERS FOR JUDICIAL SEPARATION/DIVORCE

Where a judicial separation decree has been made, along with orders relating to children, property, maintenance, etc. further orders can be sought
by either spouse in subsequent divorce proceedings that take place between them. If the spouse's financial circumstances and those of dependent children have remained largely the same since the granting of a judicial separation decree, the courts are likely to be reluctant to revise arrangements previously ordered unless the divorce decree materially alters
the financial circumstances of a spouse or dependent children.

ORDERS WHICH THE COURT CAN MAKE IN JUDICIAL
SEPARATION/DIVORCE PROCEEDINGS

Children

The court will only make a maintenance order regarding a child of a couple who is deemed to be a dependent child, i.e. who is either under the age
of 18 or is under 23 but is pursuing a full-time course of education, or
where the child suffers from a mental or physical disability that would
make it unreasonable for that child to maintain himself/herself independently.

Marital parents of children are automatically guardians of their children jointly. However, the court can only make custody and access orders
for children under the age of eighteen, i.e. directing who is to have care
and control of that child and directing access to that child for the parent
who does not have custody of the child.

Maintenance

The courts have extensive powers to order that one spouse pays maintenance to the other for that spouse's support and for the support of any

dependent members of the family. There is no such formula to determine the amount of maintenance to be paid. When making financial orders, the court takes into account a number of factors:

- the income and earning capacity of each spouse

- any other financial resources that either spouse has or is expected to have in the future

- the present and future financial needs, obligations or responsibilities of each of the spouses, including the remarriage of either spouse

- the standard of living enjoyed by the family before the application for divorce/judicial separation was made or before the spouses separated

- the age of the spouses, how long they have been married and how long they have lived together

- any physical or mental disability of either spouse

- the contribution each spouse has made, or will make, for the welfare of the family, including each spouse's contribution to the other's financial and property resources

- any contribution made by either of them in looking after the home or caring for the family

- the effect on the earning capacity of a spouse who decides not to work outside the home and the amount by which the other spouse benefited because the other did not do so

- any statutory income or benefits to which either spouse is entitled

- the accommodation needs of the spouses

- the value to each of the spouses of any benefit that one will lose by reason of divorce/judicial separation, e.g. pension benefits

- the rights of any person other than the spouses but including a person to whom either spouse is remarried

- the terms of any separation agreement still in force (only applies in the context of divorce proceedings).

At any time after the divorce/judicial separation, if there is a change of circumstances or new evidence, either party can apply to the court to vary or discharge any order for maintenance. Maintenance payments will automatically cease when the spouse receiving this payment remarries or dies.

Maintenance payments in respect of children cease when the child is no longer a dependant.

Maintenance can be ordered by the courts through making ancillary orders under the following headings:

- maintenance pending suit order

- payment order

- attachment of earnings order

- retrospective periodical payments order.

Maintenance Pending Suit Orders

Once proceedings have been issued for a decree of divorce/judicial separation, it is possible for one of the parties to apply for maintenance. When such an application has been made, the court can order maintenance payments pending the full hearing of the divorce application. The order only remains in effect until the matter is finally determined by the court at a full hearing.

Payment Orders

On the granting of divorce/judicial separation the court may make one or more of the following orders:

1. **A periodical payments order**: this can be either an order that one spouse shall make payments to the other spouse for that spouse's support or the support of any "dependent member" of the family, or the court can order that either of the spouses shall make such payments as may be specified for the benefit of any "dependent member" of the family to a third party.

2. **A lump sum order**: the court will decide the amount of such payments, the times of payments and the period during which sums are to be paid.

3. **Secured periodical payments**: the Divorce Act also makes it possible for the court to secure periodical payments orders or lump sum orders. For instance, a secured periodical payments order could direct that maintenance payments are to be deducted from rental income received from an investment property.

Attachment of Earnings Order

If a court makes a periodical payments order, it may direct that the payments are to be secured by an attachment of earnings order. This, in effect, could mean that a spouse's employer would be directed to deduct earnings from a spouse's salary to cover the periodical payments order.

A Retrospective Periodical Payments Order

When making a periodical payments order, the court can backdate it to the date of institution of proceedings, i.e. the date of the application.

The Family Home

The court will normally make one of the following orders regarding the family home:

- that one spouse would be given a right to reside in the family home for his/her life, or for such other period as the court may direct, to the exclusion of the other

- that the family home may be transferred to one of the spouses under a property adjustment order

- that the family home may be sold and the proceeds divided between the spouses. The court can direct how the proceeds of sale are to be divided and impose conditions relating to the sale.

If one spouse refuses to sign any documentation which he/she may have been ordered to sign by the court in connection with the sale of the family home, the court may direct the county registrar to sign the documentation on behalf of that spouse.

Other Assets

Depending on the circumstances of each case, a fair and proper division of these assets will be determined. If the assets are substantial, it will not be unusual to expect a lump sum payment from one spouse to the other.

Financial Compensation Orders

Such an order is designed to ensure that if the spouse who was paying maintenance dies before the other spouse, there will be sufficient money available from a pension or life policy (or both) to enable the surviving spouse to maintain himself/herself and any dependent children.

A financial compensation order can require the spouse who is ordered to provide protection to do any of the following:

- to order one or both spouses to take out life assurance or assign the benefit of an existing policy to the benefit of the other spouse or dependent member of the family
- make payments to the other spouse to enable a policy of life assurance to be made or maintained
- to divide pension entitlements for retirement and death-in-service benefits between the spouses or dependent members of the family.

Such orders shall cease to have effect on the remarriage or death of the applicant spouse insofar as they relate to the applicant.

Pension Adjustment Orders

Retirement benefits: where a decree of divorce/judicial separation has been granted, the court may, either at that time or at anytime thereafter during the lifetime of the member spouse, make a pension adjustment order providing the non-member spouse with a portion of his/her spouse's retirement benefits.

Contingent benefits: this is normally a benefit that is paid under a pension scheme on the death of the member spouse while still in employment. An order in relation to a contingent benefit shall cease to have effect if the person in whose favour the order was made dies or remarries.

Trustees: when an application is made for a pension adjustment order, the relevant trustees of the pension fund must be given notice of such an application. They are entitled to make any representations they wish and the court must take these into consideration when reaching a decision. The trustees are entitled to appear at the hearing of any application and be legally represented if they so wish. This will add substantially to the costs of such proceedings. Additionally, the level of costs incurred in obtaining all the relevant details regarding the pension could be substantial.

What is most important to realise is that only a court can make a pension adjustment order. A husband and wife cannot simply enter into a pension adjustment arrangement by agreement.

Orders for Providing for a Spouse out of the Estate of the Other Spouse (S.17)

When one party to a marriage which has ended in divorce dies, on application to the court by the other spouse, the court may make such provisions for the applicant out of the estate of the deceased spouse as it considers appropriate. This, it does while taking into account the rights of any other person with an interest in the matter.

Such applications can only be made within a period of six months after a grant of probate or administration issues. This time limit is very short and will apparently be strictly adhered to.

Before making any order, the court must also be satisfied that it was not possible to make proper provision for the applicant spouse during the lifetime of the deceased spouse by way of maintenance, property adjustment orders, financial compensation or pension adjustment orders.

An applicant spouse who has remarried since the granting of the decree of divorce cannot make an application under this section.

Domestic Violence

In the course of divorce or separation proceedings, either spouse may apply to the court for protection from the other spouse. There are various ways of doing this:

- **Protection orders**: protection orders are made on an interim or temporary basis and are often applied for in the absence of the other party. If the court is of the opinion that there are reasonable grounds for believing that the safety or welfare of the spouse or any dependent person is at risk, it may order the other spouse to refrain from frightening, molesting, using or threatening to use violence against the applicant or the dependent person.

- **Safety orders**: on hearing both sides, final relief in the form of a safety order may be granted by the court. The effect of such an order is the same as a protection order except that it is not temporary in nature.

- **Barring orders**: where the court is of the opinion that it is necessary for the safety or welfare of the applicant or any dependent person, it may prohibit the other spouse from leaving, calling to, or being present at the family home. In addition, such an order may also prohibit the frightening, molesting or use of violence against the applicant or a dependent person.

TAX PROVISIONS

Payments of money made in accordance with a court order under the Divorce Act, excluding pension adjustment orders, are to be made without deduction of income tax.

In similar circumstances to separated couples, divorced couples may agree to opt for joint assessment for income tax purposes, provided that the maintenance payer has not remarried. Therefore, for example, where there has been a divorce decree, the former husband may be granted the personal allowances and tax bands appropriate to a married person if the former wife has no income tax to pay on the maintenance payment.

Transfers of property between former spouses resulting from a court order are exempt from stamp duty.

Any transfers to a former spouse resulting from a court order are exempt from capital acquisitions tax (inheritance tax or gift tax).

The disposal of an asset from one former spouse to the other in accordance with the court order is treated on a "no gain, no loss" basis as if the former spouses were living together for capital gains tax purposes.

No probate tax is payable in respect of any provision a court might make in favour of a former spouse.

Jurisdiction of Courts

A court application may be brought in either the Circuit Family Court or the High Court. Most applications for a decree of divorce are brought in the Circuit Family Court because the legal costs are less than those in the High Court.

Under the legislation rules, the choice of the relevant Circuit Family Court where proceedings can be brought is as follows:

* the county where the spouse bringing the application ordinarily resides

* the county where the other spouse ordinarily resides

* the county where the spouse bringing the application carries on any profession, business or occupation

* the county where the other spouse carries on any profession, business or occupation.

FIRST CONSULTATION WITH A SOLICITOR

If a client is seeking advice relating to a divorce from a solicitor, it is useful to have the following information/documentation at the first meeting with the solicitor:

- marriage certificate

- any previous court orders

- any Deed of Separation or earlier agreement

- special needs of any children

- financial profile of husband and wife, including:
  - (a) employment status and income
  - (b) mortgages and debts
  - (c) properties
  - (d) current maintenance arrangements
  - (e) other assets
  - (f) pensions/life policies.

USEFUL ADDRESSES

Counsellors
Accord (Formerly CMAC)
Head Office
39 Harcourt Street
Dublin 2
Tel. 01 478 0866

Marriage and Relationship Counselling Services (MRCS)
24 Grafton Street, Dublin 2
Tel. 01 679 9341
(Non-denominational counselling.)

Irish Association of Counselling and Therapy
8 Cumberland Street
Dún Laoghaire, County Dublin
Tel. 01 230 0061

Mediators
Clanwilliam Institute
Clanwilliam Court, Dublin 6
Tel. 01 676 1363

Family Mediation Service
Block 1, Floor 5, Irish Life Centre
Lower Abbey Street, Dublin 1
Tel. 01 872 8277

Family Mediation Centre
First Floor Mill House
Henry Street, Limerick
Tel. 061 312232

Mediators' Institute Ireland (MII)
79 Merrion Square
Dublin 2
Tel. 01 661 8488

(A list of all credited mediators is available from MII.)

Legal Aid
Legal Aid Board
St Stephen's Green House
Earlsfort Terrace
Dublin 2
Tel. 01 661 5811

(A list of full-time and part-time law centres is available from the board.)

Free Legal Advice Centres
49 South William Street
Dublin 2
Tel. 01 679 4239

Coolock Community Law Centre,
Barryscourt Mall
Northside Shopping Centre
Coolock, Dublin 5
Tel. 01 847 7804 or 01 847 8602, Fax. 01 8477563

Financial Information Services Centre (FISC)
87/89 Pembroke Road
Ballsbridge
Dublin 4
Tel. 01 668 2044 or 01 668 0400

Alcoholics Anonymous
Central Office
Suite 4, 7 Donegall Street Place
Belfast BT1 2FN
Tel. 0801 232 434848

109 South Circular Road
Leonard's Corner
Dublin 8
Tel. 01 453 8998 or 01 453 7677

Al Anon Family Groups
Al Anon Information Centre
566 Capel Street
Dublin 1
Tel. 01 873 2699 (Mon.–Sat. 10.30 a.m. to 2.30 p.m.)

Gamblers Anonymous — GAM. ANON.
Carmichael House
North Brunswick Street
Dublin 7
Tel. 01 872 1133

Gingerbread Ireland
28–30 Dame Street
Dublin 2
Tel. 01 671 0291, Fax 01 671 0291 or 01 671 0352.
(Nationwide support group for one-parent families.)

Separated Persons' Association
North Brunswick Street
Dublin 7
Tel. 01 872 0684

The Samaritans
112 Marlborough Street
Dublin 1
Tel. 01 872 7700
Helpline: 1850-60-90-90

Women's Aid
Freephone Helpline: 1800 341 900

Accord
Head Office
All Hallowes College
Drumcondra
Dublin 9
Tel. 01 837 1151
(Administration Headquarters of Accord, the Nationwide Counselling Organisation.)

Aim Family Services

6 D'Olier Street
Dublin 2
Tel. 01 670 8363

National Social Service Board

7th Floor
Hume House
Ballsbridge
Dublin 4
Tel. 01 605 9000

Department of Social, Community and Family Affairs

One-Parent Family Section
College Road
Sligo
Tel. 01 704 3376 (for Dublin callers) or 071 69800

Revenue Central Telephone Information Office

Tel. 01 878 0000 (For tax and information.)

Chapter Ten

Medical Treatment

CONSENT TO TREATMENT

A doctor cannot compel his patient to accept treatment however convinced he may be that it is in the patient's best interests. No medical treatment should be given without the consent of the patient. Nevertheless, the question has to be asked: In what circumstances is the patient competent to give that consent and to what extent should the views or wishes of relatives and carers be taken into account?

There are situations where the patient is not competent enough to consent to treatment that could be given and which the doctor considers is needed or desirable. That treatment may be needed in an emergency or in order to preserve the life of the patient, or it may be the kind of treatment that is a matter of personal choice. In what circumstances can the doctor proceed with the treatment without the patient's knowledge or approval?

No medical treatment should be given without the consent of the patient. However, consent may be implied, as when the patient presents himself for treatment, though even then it may be only a diagnosis that is requested. The Irish law relating to consent to treatment by patients was set out in the following paragraphs of the judgement of Mrs Justice Denham of 27 July 1995 in the case referred to as *In re a Ward of Court*:

> Medical treatment may not be given to an adult person of full capacity without his or her consent. There are a few rare exceptions to this, e.g. in regard to contagious diseases or in a medical emergency where the patient is unable to communicate. This right arises out of civil, criminal and constitutional law. If medical treatment is given without consent it may be a trespass against the person in civil law, a battery in criminal law and a breach of the individual's constitutional rights. The consent which is given by an adult of full capacity is a matter of choice. It is not necessarily a decision based on medical consideration. Thus, medical treatment may be refused for other than medical reasons. Such reasons may not be viewed as good

medical reasons, or reasons most citizens would regard as rational, but a person of full age and capacity may make decisions for their own reasons.

If the patient is a minor then consent may be given on their behalf by parents or guardians. If the patient is incapacitated by reason other than age then the issue of capacity to consent arises. In this instance, where the patient is a ward of court, the court makes a decision.

Capacity to Consent to Treatment

Determining whether a person is competent for the purposes of consenting to medical treatment is not a straightforward matter. It may be one of degree, depending on the reasons why the procedure is deemed necessary and the extent to which the patient can understand that necessity, taking into account all the essential issues. The complexity of the proposed treatment and the degree of understanding required will be different in each case. Capacity should therefore be assessed on each occasion and be continually reassessed with each particular treatment and at each stage of treatment.

Incompetent Patients

Often, when a patient is unconscious and incapable of consenting, hospital staff will consult the relatives of the patient. In strict legal terms, however, the consent of the patient's relatives to a particular procedure has no validity and the real legal issue for the medical staff is whether or not there is an immediate necessity for the procedure in question.

The extent to which a doctor is under a duty to comply with the previously expressed wishes of a patient raises complex issues, but there is no clear answer in Irish law to this dilemma. If the patient has expressly envisaged at some prior time a particular medical eventuality, and leaves instructions that a particular treatment is not to be given, a doctor may be legally obliged to refrain from treatment despite the consequences of that course of action.

Medical Treatment of Seriously Ill Persons

The existing Irish law was summarised in the High Court judgement of Mr Justice Lynch of 5 May 1995 in the Ward of Court case. The following principles enunciated by Judge Lynch were not specifically approved in the Supreme Court judgements but neither were they stated to be incorrect. In his judgement, Judge Lynch set out the following principles:

> As I understand the medical evidence, the present practice by the medical and nursing professions in relation to patients is as follows and is a lawful and proper practice:
>
> 1. A competent terminally ill patient is lawfully entitled to require that life-support systems be either withdrawn or not provided as the case may be.
>
> 2. In the case of an incompetent terminally ill patient, the carers, in agreement with appropriate surrogates, be they family or friends, bona fide acting in what they believe to be the best interests of the patient, may lawfully withdraw or refrain from providing life-support systems.
>
> 3. In the case of incompetent terminally ill patients, where the carers believe such assistance should be withdrawn or not provided but the surrogates disagree, a second medical opinion should be obtained from a suitably qualified independent medical practitioner. If his opinion agrees with the carers, they may lawfully act accordingly, preferably having got the agreement of the surrogates with the aid of such second opinion; if his opinion agrees with the surrogates, the appropriate life-support systems should be maintained or provided, as the case may be.
>
> 4. In the case of an incompetent patient, whether terminally ill or not, where the surrogates believe that life-support systems should either be withdrawn or not provided and the carers disagree, such systems should be maintained or provided unless an order of the High Court to the contrary is obtained by the surrogates.

WARD OF COURT CASE

The only court decision in Ireland in this area concerned a ward of court who was not competent to make any decisions. In a landmark decision (in *re a Ward of Court*) on 27 July 1995 the full Supreme Court (by a four to one majority) upheld the earlier High Court judgement (of Judge Lynch) consenting (on the application of the ward's family) to the withdrawal and termination of abnormal artificial means of nourishment from a ward of court in a near permanent vegetative state (PVS), thus ceasing to prolong her life.

The ward in this case was a woman in her mid-forties who some 23 years previously suffered very serious brain damage in the course of what should have been a routine gynaecological operation. Since then, she had been near PVS in an Irish hospital where she had been kept alive by means of a life-support feeding system.

In its deliberations, the Supreme Court considered whether the personal rights protected by the Constitution would include the right to refuse medical care or treatment and whether the right to life included the right to die a natural death (as opposed to having life terminated or death accelerated). The court decided that the ward's personal rights were not lessened or diminished by her incapacity, and that the responsibility for their exercise and vindication rested with the court (rather than the next of kin) to make the decision, with the first and paramount consideration being the well-being, welfare and interests of the ward. The Supreme Court majority accepted that the true cause of death in the event of withdrawal of nourishment would be the original injuries sustained.

The Supreme Court decision, even though grounded on the Irish Constitution, gave consideration to precedents from other common law jurisdictions where the issue of withdrawal of a life-support feeding system had been addressed. It appears that such decisions in those other jurisdictions have not resulted in a flood of court applications.

The legal kernel of the decision may be summarised as follows:

1. That in certain circumstances the (ward of court) patient who is fully PVS or near PVS may have artificial food and hydration withdrawn by order of court where there is no prospect of improvement, so that the patient can be allowed to die naturally, provided that the court decides that it is in the patient's best interests for this to happen.

2. That no such order can be made which might affect the old, the infirm or the mentally handicapped, although the dividing line between these categories of patient and a near PVS patient did not arise for a decision in the case.

3. While Judge Lynch (in the High Court) and Judge Denham (in her individual Supreme Court judgement) considered possible guidelines which could be followed by the courts in future cases, the overall majority decision did not lay down any such guidelines other than that the future decisions would have to be made with regard to the individual facts of each case.

During the course of its judgement, the Supreme Court discussed whether a "substituted judgement" test could be used. This means that the court puts itself in the place of the incompetent patient and decides what he or she would have wished in the particular circumstances. In the Ward of Court case, the Supreme Court did not follow this approach but it appears that this was largely because of the fact that there was insufficient evidence as to what the ward's views would have been on the matter. However, given the Supreme Court's emphasis on the importance of personal autonomy, it may be that where an incompetent person's views are clearly expressed these would be given considerable weight by the court in future cases. This highlights the potential importance of "advance directives", which are considered below.

ADVANCE DIRECTIVES/LIVING WILLS

It is possible for persons to set out their views regarding future medical care by way of what are known as advance directives (also known as living wills). There is no legislation in relation to advance directives in Ireland and the legal position is quite unclear. An advance directive is basically a document whereby a person sets out the basis on which health care decisions should be made if he or she becomes mentally incapable or unable to participate in those decisions.

For instance, the document might include the request that certain treatment should or should not be given in certain situations if the person is not competent to consent to or refuse such treatment at the time.

Obviously, an advance directive can only relate to lawful treatment (such as the withdrawal of medical treatment) and cannot relate to unlawful treatment, such as giving a lethal injection with no therapeutic effect and with the intention of terminating life.

Certain comments by members of the Supreme Court in the Ward of Court case suggested that the views expressed by a person in relation to future medical treatment (which could be set out in an advance directive) would be taken into account by the court in coming to decisions in relation to the termination of treatment. Nevertheless, the context to which these views relate and the extent to which they would be binding on medical professionals remains unclear.

In addition, there are of course, issues about how specific advance directives can be given, the considerable variation and the types of medical intervention which are now possible. In view of the uncertainties involved, a person wishing to draw up an advance directive (or living will) should seek both details and legal advice from his/her solicitor and discuss it with his/her doctor.

Sample Living Will

This Living Will

is made on the _____ day of _____ 20
by me _____
of _____
born on _____

I wish these instructions to be acted upon if two registered medical practitioners are of the opinion that I am no longer capable of making and communicating a treatment decision *and* that I am:

- unconscious and it is unlikely that I shall ever regain consciousness

- suffering from an incurable or irreversible condition that will result in my death within a relatively short time

- so severely disabled, physically or mentally, that I shall be totally dependent on others for the rest of my life.

I refuse any medical or surgical treatment if:

- its burdens and risks outweigh its potential benefits

- it involves any research or experimentation which is likely to be of little or no therapeutic value to me

- it will needlessly prolong my life or postpone the actual moment of my death.

I consent to being fed orally and to any treatment that may:

- safeguard my dignity

- make me more comfortable

- relieve pain and suffering, even though such treatment might unintentionally precipitate my death.

Signed by me _____

in the presence of _____

Name _____

Address _____

Occupation _____

Chapter Eleven

Enforcing Legal Rights Cheaply

SMALL CLAIMS COURT

The Small Claims Court is part of the District Court and was set up to deal with consumer complaints speedily, cheaply and informally. It is confined to cases where the value of the claim is not more than £1,000. The procedure for making claims costs £6 and is quite straightforward. It is not necessary to have legal representation. The court is located in District Court No. 54, in the Old Richmond Hospital, North Brunswick Street, Dublin 7. The telephone number to contact is 8725555.

An application is made to the Small Claims Registrar, a registrar of the District Court, who will deal with consumer claims in relation to any goods or services purchased. The procedure also includes minor damage and rent deposits but is not available for use by one businessperson against another.

Claims with regard to accidents/personal injuries or for the recovery of payments under a loan or hire purchase agreement are excluded, but claims concerning goods bought on credit are included. In short, claims could be made for bad workmanship and faulty goods as far as most everyday transactions for goods and services are concerned but not for debts or personal injuries.

There is a free Small Claims Court advice service available through the European Consumer Advice Centre at 13a O'Connell Street, Dublin 1. Alternatively, the Small Claims Registrar (or his/her staff) will help with advice and filling in the application form to make your claim. The Office of the Director of Consumer Affairs will also give advice (Tel. 4025555). You can also obtain information from your local Citizen's Information Centre.

The completed application form, together with the fee of £6, is lodged with the Small Claims Registrar. A copy of the application form would be sent to the person against whom the claim is made (i.e. the respondent). The original application form will be kept in the office of the Registrar.

If the Small Claims Registrar receives a notice from the respondent disputing your claim or making a counter-claim against you, the Registrar will contact you and let you have a copy of the respondent's answer. The Registrar may interview both parties and/or invite both parties to discuss the claim together with him/her to try and reach an agreement.

If the respondent admits your claim, he/she will notify the Registrar's office by returning the acceptance of liability form. If within fifteen days of receiving a copy of your application the respondent does not reply, the claim will be automatically treated as undisputed and the District Court will make an order in your favour for the amount claimed to be paid within four weeks usually.

If the claim is disputed, the Small Claims Registrar will attempt to bring about a settlement. If this fails, he/she will bring the case to the District Court for a hearing. The initial fee will cover the cost of the court hearing.

The meeting will be informal and private. The Small Claims Registrar will probably ask you and the respondent to outline the facts. He/she may question both parties in an effort to clarify the issues. If an agreement cannot be reached, the Registrar may fix a date, time and location there and then for a hearing of the claim before a judge of the District Court. The date and time of the hearing and the address of the courthouse will be sent to both parties by post.

In the District Court the Registrar will outline the alleged facts (and any counter-claim) to the court. He/she will put any agreed facts before the court. He/she will then call you to give evidence. The judge will ask you to tell your version of the facts and may question you directly. The same arrangement will apply to the respondent.

If the matter is resolved in your favour, the respondent will be notified of the court's decision a few days after the hearing and will be allowed about four weeks to pay the amount awarded by the court.

The respondent should pay you the amount of the award within a reasonable time, but if he/she does not, you can apply to the Small Claims Registrar to have the order of the court enforced by the sheriff. Information and assistance regarding enforcement procedures are available from the Small Claims Registrar.

All the above information is available in a guide to small claims in the District Court issued by the Department of Justice, Equality and Law Reform. Copies of the guide are also available from your local District Court.

THE OMBUDSMAN

The Ombudsman's main function is to investigate complaints from members of the public who feel they have been unfairly treated by certain public bodies, namely government departments and offices, local authorities, health boards and An Post.

The Ombudsman has extensive powers in law. He can demand any information, document or file from a body complained of and he can require any official to give information about a complaint. He can look into all administrative actions including decisions, refusal to take action and administrative procedures. Before you contact the Ombudsman, you must first try to solve your problem with the public body concerned. If you fail to resolve your problem and you feel that the body concerned has not treated you fairly, you may contact the Ombudsman.

Complaints may be made in writing, by telephone or by calling to the Ombudsman's office at 18 Lower Leeson Street, Dublin 2 (Tel. 1890 223030, Fax. 01 661 0570).

The Ombudsman does not charge for dealing with complaints. He/she will have his staff examine the complaint to see if it is justified. In the majority of cases, complaints are resolved satisfactorily in a very informal way, e.g. by discussing the problem with the public body or by examining the relevant files. In the more complex cases, a detailed investigation may be required.

If the Ombudsman finds that your complaint is wholly or partly justified, he will report this to the department or public body concerned. He may recommend that it should review its action or change its decision.

The Ombudsman has no power to force a body to act on or accept his recommendation. If it does not, he may find it necessary to make a report on the matter to the Houses of the Oireachtas.

All the of above information is contained in a booklet which may be obtained from the Office of the Ombudsman.

THE INFORMATION COMMISSIONER

The Information Commissioner's job is to provide an independent avenue of appeal for members of the public who are not happy with decisions made by public bodies in relation to information requested under the Freedom of Information Act 1997 (hereafter the "FOI").

The FOI Act 1997 grants you the following new legal rights:

1. To access information held by public bodies.

2. To have personal information about you held by these bodies and corrected or updated where necessary.

3. To be given reasons for decisions taken by public bodies that affect you.

These rights are subject to certain exceptions, but in general you can look for records created after 21 April 1998 and for personal information held about you, no matter when it was created.

Most appeals to the Commissioner originate from refusals by public bodies to provide access to records. However, the Commissioner can also review:

- a refusal to provide the record (e.g. where only access is given to records or where the records are only given on computer disk and a hard copy is not supplied)

- a postponement to a later date of access to the record

- a refusal to correct or update personal information

- a refusal to give reasons for a decision of the public body which affects the person

- the fee or deposit charged by the public body for access to information

- a proposal to release personal information and confidential information or commercially sensitive information, despite third-party objections.

If you are unhappy with the decision of a public body in relation to your FOI request, you must first ask for a review of the decision by a more senior person within the body. If you are still dissatisfied, you may then appeal to the Information Commissioner. Public bodies are required to give reasonable help to people in making their request. However, if you are not sure that you have been properly dealt with by the public body, you may contact the Information Commissioner's office for advice.

In most cases, you must appeal to the Commissioner for a review of the final decision of a public body within six months of notification. The Commissioner can agree or differ with all the decisions of the body. He can also try to effect a settlement between the parties. Appeals are normally completed within four months.

There is no charge for dealing with appeals to the Commissioner. Nevertheless, public bodies are entitled to charge fees and deposits for access to information.

The Commissioner's decision on appeals is binding and conclusive. There is a right of appeal to the High Court regarding the Commissioner's decision, but only on a point of law.

The Information Commissioner *cannot* review decisions made by private companies or individuals or decisions made by public bodies which are not covered by the Act.

All government departments, local authorities and health boards are covered by the FOI Act. Some executive agencies in government departments are also covered by the Act. Other public bodies may be brought within the scope of the Act at a future date.

If you have a query on FOI or wish to appeal an FOI decision, contact the Office of the Information Commissioner, 18 Lower Leeson Street, Dublin 2 (Tel. 1890-22-30-30 (local call rate), Fax: 01 661 0570).

CIVIL LEGAL AID

The Civil Legal Aid Scheme is not a free legal aid scheme. It is administered by the Legal Aid Board, which provides legal aid advice in civil cases to persons who satisfy the requirements of the Civil Legal Aid Act 1995. The Board makes the services of solicitors and, if necessary, barristers available to people of moderate means at little cost.

The service includes anything from writing a solicitor's letter on your behalf to representing you in court proceedings.

The Civil Legal Aid Scheme can help you with such legal matters as:

- legal separations

- maintenance

- barring

- custody of children

- divorce

- a problem about hire purchase

- a landlord and tenant dispute

- a contract.

Quite a few areas are excluded from the scope of the Civil Legal Aid Scheme. Excluded areas include:

- criminal proceedings: there is a separate criminal legal aid scheme

- defamation: there are some exceptions

- debt collection: where a person in difficulties with a moneylender may be able to get legal aid

- disputes over land: again, there are some exceptions
- civil bills for amounts under £150
- arbitration under the Landlord and Tenant Acts
- conveyancing, i.e. buying or selling property
- licensing: again, with some exceptions
- election petitions
- cases coming before tribunals: cases before the Employment Appeals Tribunal and Social Welfare Appeals Tribunal (income tax appeals are not covered by the scheme)
- proceedings which could probably be brought in the Small Claims Court.

You can apply at any one of the law centres throughout the country. There are full-time law centres in practically every main city and part-time law centres elsewhere. The addresses and telephone numbers of all the law centres can be provided by the Legal Aid Board, St Stephen's Green House, Earlsfort Terrace, Dublin 2 (Tel. 01 661 5811, Fax. 01 676 3426).

If you depend on social welfare payments, you qualify at the minimum rate provided that you satisfy the criteria laid down in the FOI Act.

If you are working, it depends on your "disposable" income, i.e. what you have left after certain allowances are made for dependants, rent, mortgage repayments, expenses in travelling to work, hire purchase repayments and various other outgoing payments. The present eligibility limit is £7,350 per annum in disposable income.

If you depend on social welfare payments, the most it will cost you is £4 for legal advice and £23 if you go to court. If your disposable income exceeds £5,060 per annum, you are required to pay a larger contribution up to a maximum of £595.

If it becomes necessary to go to court, the value of the applicant's capital resources (e.g. house, land, money in a bank, car, etc.) is also taken into account and a capital contribution may be payable. However, capital contributions arise in very few cases.

The above information has been furnished from booklets published by the Legal Aid Board.

THE INSURANCE OMBUDSMAN OF IRELAND

The Insurance Ombudsman deals with complaints between members of the public and an insurance company. Before the Ombudsman can adjudicate on a dispute, it is necessary for the policyholder to process the complaint, dispute or claim through the insurance company's complaint procedure.

All of the insurance companies participating in the Ombudsman scheme have nominated a member of senior management whose responsibility it is to "sign off" your dispute if it fails to settle. If you are not satisfied by the explanation or offer made by the insurance company, then you may refer the matter to the Insurance Ombudsman for consideration.

Being able to refer your dispute to the Ombudsman is subject to the following conditions:

1. You, the complainant, are the person who took out the policy which is the subject of the dispute.

2. Your dispute or claim has been processed through the insurance company's internal complaints procedures and the company has confirmed in writing that no agreed settlement has resulted.

3. You refer your dispute to the Ombudsman within six months of having received written confirmation from the company that no settlement has resulted.

4. You have not initiated court proceedings or referred the dispute to arbitration or to the Minister for Enterprise and Employment.

5. The amount in dispute must be £100,000 or less and if the policy concerns permanent health, the basic benefits insured must amount to £10,000 or less per annum.

Outlined below are some of the matters the Insurance Ombudsman *cannot* consider:

• where any dispute about life assurance concerns the actuarial standards, tables and principles which your insurance company applies to its ordinary or industrial long-term insurance business, including the method of calculation of surrender of values, paid-up policy values, the bonus system and the bonus rates applicable to the policy in question

• disputes or claims between a complainant and any other person other than the complainant's insurance company

• disputes or questions relating to any acts or omissions of any insurance intermediary other than those for which the member insurance company bears full legal responsibility, including acts or omissions of tied insurance agents

- a matter which would be more appropriately dealt with by a court of law
- a matter barred by law because the time in bringing the action had expired.

If the Ombudsman adjudicates on the matter and makes an award, you are free to accept or reject it. On the other hand, the member assurance companies have agreed to be bound by the Ombudsman's decision. In the event of you accepting the offer or award, you must do so in full and final settlement of your claim against the company. If you are not satisfied with the decision of the Ombudsman you can reject it and pursue another course of redress, either by arbitration or through the court. You cannot, of course, accept an award from the Ombudsman and then take legal action. It is important to note that if the Ombudsman has not upheld your claim, you have not prejudiced any of your legal rights by referring the matter to the Ombudsman. All the above information has been provided by brochures distributed by the Insurance Ombudsman of Ireland, 32 Upper Merrion Street, Dublin 2 (Tel. 01 662 0899).

INSURANCE INFORMATION SERVICE

The Irish Insurance Federation provides a free insurance information service (IIS) where you can obtain information and advice on all aspects of insurance. This service will also investigate complaints that fall outside the scope of the Insurance Ombudsman scheme. In particular, it will assist anyone who is unable to obtain a quotation for motor insurance and will arrange for his or her case to be considered under the terms of the Declined Cases Agreement. You may contact the Free Information Service/ Insurance Information Service/Irish Insurance Federation, 39 Molesworth Street, Dublin 2 (Tel. 01 676 1820).

DEPARTMENT OF ENTERPRISE, TRADE AND EMPLOYMENT

The primary role of the Department is to ensure that insurance companies authorised to operate in the marketplace meet their statutory reserve and solvency requirements. The insurance complaints section of the Department deals with complaints/queries from policyholders and other members of the public, although there is no statutory obligation to resolve insurance complaints. The Department of Enterprise, Trade and Employment is located at Kildare Street, Dublin 2 (Tel. 01 661 4444).

Appendix

List of Organisations Working for Older People

No.	Name	Address	Tel No.	Other Information
1.	Age Action Ireland	30/31 Lr. Camden St. Dublin 2	4785060	Works as a network of organisations and people providing services for older people and their carers and promotes better policies and services for them.
2.	Irish Senior Citizens' Parliament	56 Parnell Square West, Dublin 1	8782541/2	To give a voice to senior citizens regarding the issues that affect the quality of their lives.
3.	Age and Opportunity	Marino Institute of Education St Joseph's Building Griffith Avenue Dublin 9	8370570	It aims to work to encourage and enable older people to participate fully in the community.
4.	Alzheimer Society of Ireland	Alzheimer House 43 Northumberland Avenue Dún Laoghaire County Dublin	2846616	
5.	Alzheimer Care Centre	Highfield Private Hospital Swords Road Dublin 9	8374444	
6.	Alzheimer Day Care Centre	St Teresa's Temple Hill Blackrock County Dublin	2887572	
7.	Carers' Association	St Mary's Community Centre, Richmond Hill Rathmines Dublin 6	4974498/ 4974148 Freephone: 1800 240714	To support and represent carers.
8.	Caring for Carers in Ireland	Barefield Ennis County Clare	0656 821313	To promote the well-being of family carers in Ireland.
9.	Council for Social Welfare	169 Booterstown Ave. Blackrock County Dublin	2887068	

No.	Name	Address	Tel No.	Other Information
10.	Federation of Active Retire-ment Assoc.	59/61 Dame St. Dublin 2	6792142	
11.	Irish Society of Chartered Physiotherapists	Royal College of Surgeons St Stephen's Green, Dublin 2	4022148	
12.	Care Alliance Ireland	30/31 Lwr Camden St. Dublin 2	4756989	National network of voluntary organisations for carers.
13.	Irish Association of Older People	Room GO2 University College Earlsfort Terrace Dublin 2	4750013	
14.	Irish College of General Practitioners	4 Lincoln Place Dublin 2	6763705	
15.	Irish Hospice Foundation	9 Fitzwilliam Place Dublin 2	6765599	
16.	Irish Society of. Physicians in Geriatric Med	Adelaide and Meath Hospital Incorporating INCH, Tallaght Dublin 24	4142000	
17.	National Council on Ageing and Older People	22 Clanwilliam Square Grand Canal Quay Dublin 2	6766484	
18.	National Rehabilitation Board	25 Clyde Road Dublin 4	6684181	
19.	Retirement Planning Council of Ireland	27/29 Lr. Pembroke St. Dublin 2	6613139	
20.	Society of St Vincent de Paul	8 New Cabra Road Dublin 7	8384164	
21.	National Asso-ciation of Home Help Organisers (NAHHO)	42 Slieve Rua Drive Stillorgan Co. Dublin	2886393	Assists people in looking after the elderly in their own homes.
22.	National Association of Widows in Ireland	12 Upper Ormond Quay Dublin 7	6770977/ 6770513	
23.	Association of Occupational Therapists in Ireland (AOTI)	4 Greenmount Office Park, Harolds Cross Dublin 6W	4730320	
24.	Irish Institute of Pension Managers (IIPM)	39 Molesworth St. Dublin 2	6620320	

No.	Name	Address	Tel No.	Other Information
25.	Irish Nursing Homes' Organisation	2012 Citywest Business Campus Naas Road Saggart County Dublin	4660185	
26.	CrossCare	The Red House Clonliffe College Dublin 3	8360011	Includes an information and advice service regarding entitlements for older people and carers.
27.	Our Lady's Hospice	Box 222 Harold's Cross Dublin 6W	4972101	
28.	Irish Association of Social Workers	St Andrews Resource Centre, 114 Pearse St. Dublin 2	6774838	
29.	Irish Hospitals Consultants' Association	Heritage House Main St. Dundrum Dublin 14	2989123	
30.	Medical Council	Lynn House Portobello Court Lower Rathmines Rd Dublin 6	4965588	
31.	Care for the Elderly at Home Ltd.	14 South Leinster St. Dublin 2	6623423	
32.	Friends of the Elderly	25 Bolton St. Dublin 1	8731855	Organises visits to the elderly in their home or in hospital.
33.	Irish Countrywomen's Association	58 Merrion Road Dublin 4	6680452	
34.	National Asso-ciation of Home Care Organisers	Kilbarrack Health Centre Dublin 5	8391221	
35.	The Pensions Board	2nd Floor Holbrook House Holles St. Dublin 2	6762622	
36.	Citizen Informa-tion Centre	O'Connell St. CIS Consumer Advice Shop 13A Upp. O'Connell St. Dublin 1	8090633	(developed by the Citizens' Information Development Project)
37.	Energy Action	Unit 14 IDA Centre Newmarket Dublin 8	4545464	
38.	Reach Out Family Support Group	Resource Centre Killinarden Way Dublin 24	4625255	Encourages people to help elderly neighbours.

No.	Name	Address	Tel No.	Other Information
39.	The Office of the Ombudsman	Ossory House Lower Leeson St. Dublin 2	6785222	Investigates complaints against certain public bodies.
40.	National Social Services Board	7th Floor Hume House Ballsbridge Dublin 4	6059000	National registered body of Citizen Information Services. It is a public service body which provides information and access to social services.
41.	Victim Support	29/30 Dame St. Dublin 2	6798673	To help people come to terms with the experience of being a victim of crime.
42.	Irish Widowers' and Deserted Husbands' Association	54 Foster Terrace Ballybough Dublin 3	8552334	
43.	Minus One	68 Lower Leeson St. Dublin 2	6765596	Support group for separated and bereaved persons.
44.	Disability Federation of Ireland	2 Sandyford Office Pk Dublin 18	2959344	
45.	Forum of People with Disabilities	21 Hill St. Dublin 1	8786077	
46.	Care for Dublin's Old Folk Living Alone	Carmichael House North Brunswick St. Dublin 7	8735702	
47.	Protestant Aid	74 Upper Leeson St. Dublin 2	6684298	
48.	Department of Health (Services for Older People)	Hawkins House Hawkins St. Dublin 2	6354000	
49.	Irish Nurses' Organisation	11 Fitzwilliam Place Dublin 2	6760137	
50.	Retirement Association of Home Information Services Ltd.	158 Stillorgan Road Donnybrook Dublin 4	2691832	Provides information about nursing homes and details of any vacancies.

CITIZENS' INFORMATION CENTRES

CIC = Citizens' Information Centre
FISC = Financial Information Services Centre
FLAC = Free Legal Advice Centre

No.	Area	Address	Tel. No.
Dublin			
1.	Balbriggan Community College	Drogheda St., Balbriggan, County Dublin	01 841 4600
2.	Ballymun CIC	Library, Ballymun Road, Dublin 9	01 842 1890
3.	Blanchardstown CIC	Roselawn Health Centre, Blanchardstown, Dublin 15	01 822 0449
	Also at Mountview	Health Centre, Shelerin Road, Clonsilla, Dublin 15	
4.	Cabra CIC (CIDP)	1a St Eithne's Road, Cabra, Dublin 7	01 868 5945
5.	CIC (Centre for the Deaf)	40 Lower Drumcondra Road, Dublin 9	01 830 5744
6.	City Centre Information Centre (CIDP)	Consumer Advice Shop, 13a O'Connell St., Dublin 1	01 809 0633
7.	Clondalkin CIC	Unit 2, Oakfield Industrial Estate, 9th Lock Road, Clondalkin, Dublin 22	01 457 0861
8.	Crumlin CIC	146 Sundrive Road, Crumlin, Dublin 12	01 454 6070/ 454 6080
9.	Also at Dolphin's Barn	Dolphin's Barn Library, Dolphin's Barn, Dublin 8	
10.	Rathmines	221 Lower Rathmines Road, Dublin 6	01 496 5558
11.	Walkinstown	Walkinstown Library, Walkinstown, Dublin 12	
12.	Donnycarney/Beaumont CIC	Social Service Centre, St John's Court, Donnycarney, Dublin 9	01 831 9783
13.	Dundrum CIC	Dom Marmion House, Sandyford Road, Dundrum, Dublin 14	01 296 0713
14.	Dún Laoghaire CIC	85/86 Patrick St., Dún Laoghaire, County Dublin	01 284 4544
15.	Finglas CIC	7 Main St., Finglas, Dublin 11	01 864 1970
16.	Finglas South	St Helena's Resource Centre	01 836 2658
17.	Finglas West	Barry's Shopping Mall	01 864 3863
18.	Killester CIC	Social Services Centre, 2 Sybil Hill Road, Killester, Dublin 5	01 831 3700

No.	Area	Address	Tel. No.
19.	Ardlea	Ardlea Parish Centre, Ardlea Church Grounds	
20.	Lucan CIC	Town Hall, Lucan, County Dublin	01 624 1975
21.	Malahide CIC	Library Car Park, Malahide, County Dublin	01 845 0627
22.	Donaghmede	Library, Donaghmede Shopping Centre	
23.	Markets Area CIC	MACRO Resource Centre, 22 Beresford St., Dublin 7	01 872 0521
24.	National Association for Deaf People	35 North Frederick St., Dublin 1	01 872 3800
25.	Palmerstown CIC	Parish Centre, Kennelsfort Road, Palmerstown, Dublin 20	01 626 3050
26.	Rialto CIC	Rialto Parish Centre, Old National School, SCR, Dublin	01 453 9965
27.	SICCDA-Liberties CIC	90 Meath St., Dublin 8	01 453 6098
28.	Skerries CIC	Strand House Clinic, Strand St., Skerries, County Dublin	01 849 4443
29.	Stillorgan CIC	St Laurence's Community Centre, Lower Kilmacud Road, Stillorgan, County Dublin	01 288 5629
30	Swords CIC	"Ormonde", 58 Dublin Road, Swords, County Dublin	01 840 6877
31.	Tallaght CIC	1 Main St., Tallaght, Dublin 24	01 451 5911
32.	The Square, Tallaght	Community Information Desk, Level 3, The Square, Tallaght, Dublin 24	
33.	Whitehall/Beaumont CIC	Pastoral Centre, Montrose Park, Dublin 5	01 847 7118
	Connaught/Ulster		
1.	**Cavan**	Dublin Road, Cavan	049 433 2641
	Cavan MABS		049 62900
	Donegal		
1.	Ballyshannon CIC	Day Centre, College St., Ballyshannon, County Donegal	072 51666
2.	Buncrana CIC	2 Victoria Villas, St Mary's Road, Buncrana, County Donegal	077 63496
3.	Letterkenny CIC	Resource Centre, Pearse Road, Letterkenny, County Donegal	074 27177
4.	Lifford	New Resource Centre, Lifford, County Donegal	

No.	Area	Address	Tel. No.
	Galway		
1.	Galway CIC	Augustine House, St Augustince St., Galway	091 563344
2.	Clifden	Library Building, Market St., Clifden, County Galway	095 22000
3.	Cornamona		092 48031
4.	Rosmuc		091 574122
5.	Tuam CIC	Social Service Centre, Dublin Road, Tuam, Co. Galway	093 24577
	Mayo		
1.	Ballina CIC	Community Centre, Teeling St., Ballina, County Mayo	096 21221
2.	Erris	The Square, Belmullet, Co. Mayo	094 81676
3.	Castlebar CIC	Social Service Centre, Castle St., Castlebar, County Mayo	094 21880
4.	Claremorris CIC	Social Service Centre, Dalton St., Claremorris, County Mayo	094 62096
	Monaghan		
1.	Monaghan CIC	9 Market St., Monaghan	047 82622
	Roscommon		
1.	Boyle CIC	St Patrick St., Boyle, Co. Roscommon	079 62986
2.	Ballaghadereen		
3.	Castlerea		
	Sligo		
1.	Sligo CIC Co. Ltd.	7/8 John St., Sligo	071 51133/ 41737
	Munster		
	Clare		
1.	Ennis CIC	Harmony Row, Ennis, County Clare	065 6841221
2.	Shannon CIC	c/o Business Centre, Shannon Town Centre, Shannon, Co. Clare	061 364704/5
	County Cork		
1.	Bantry CIC	Community Resource Centre, Glengarriff Road, Bantry	027 52100
2.	Skibbereen	Sutherland Centre, North St., Skibbereen, County Cork	

No.	Area	Address	Tel. No.
2.	Portlaoise CIC	4 Peppers Court, Portlaoise, County Laois	0502 21425
	Longford		
1.	Family Centre	St Mel's Road, Longford	043 41069
	Louth		
1.	Drogheda CIC	Community Services Centre, Fair St., Drogheda, County Louth	041 36084
2.	Dundalk CIC	Social Services Centre, Clanbrassil St., Dundalk, County Louth	042 32848
	Meath		
1.	Ashbourne CIC	Youth Centre, Main St., Ashbourne, County Meath	01 8351806
2.	Navan CIC	1 Brews Hill, Navan, County Meath	046 74086
			Freephone: 1800 206 506
3.	Trim CIC	Enterprise Centre, Riverbank, Trim, County Meath	046 36349
	Offaly		
1.	Edenderry CIC	Edenderry Business Park, St Mary's St., Edenderry, County Offaly	0405 32733
2.	Tullamore CIC	18 Chapel St., Tullamore, County Offaly	0506 52204
	Westmeath		
1.	Athlone CIC	St Mary's Place, Athlone, County Westmeath	0902 78851
2.	Mullingar CIC	Social Service Centre, Bishopsgate St., Mullingar, County Westmeath	044 40700
	Wexford		
1.	Enniscorthy CIC	Athenaeum, Enniscorthy, County Wexford	054 33746
2.	Wexford	St Bridget's Centre, Roches Road, Wexford	053 23301
	Wicklow		
1.	Arklow CIC	Portocabin, Quinnsworth Car Park, Arklow, County Wicklow	0402 32411
2.	Bray CIC	Health Centre, Killarney Road, Bray, County Wicklow	01 2869590
3.	Greystones	Quinnsworth Shopping Centre, Greystones, County Wicklow	01 2871027

HEALTH BOARDS

1. **Eastern Health Board**
   Dr Steeven's Hospital
   Dublin 8
   Tel. 01 6790700
   Customer Services Department — Freephone: 1800 520 520

2. **Midland Health Board**
   Arden Road
   Tullamore
   County Offaly
   Tel. 0506/21868

3. **Mid-Western Health Board**
   31/33 Catherine St.
   Limerick
   Tel. 061 316655

4. **North Eastern Health Board**
   Kells
   County Meath
   Tel. 046 40341

5. **North Western Health Board**
   Manorhamilton
   County Leitrim
   Tel. 072 20400

6. **South Eastern Health Board**
   Lacken
   Dublin Road
   Kilkenny
   Tel. 056 51702

7. **Southern Health Board**
   Cork Farm Centre
   Western Road
   Cork
   Tel. 021 545011

8. **Western Health Board**
   Merlin Park Regional Hospital
   Galway
   Tel. 091 751131

Glossary

Abatement: Abatement is the pro rata diminution of a legacy where the estate is insufficient to meet it in full.

Additional Voluntary Contributions (AVCs): Most pension schemes will allow employees to improve their retirement benefits by making Additional Voluntary Contributions (AVCs) in any tax year. These are subject to the total employee contributions not exceeding 15 per cent of gross pay in any year for an occupational pension.

Ademption: If the subject matter of a specific legacy has ceased to exist on the testator's death, or has been so altered that it no longer exists in the form described in the will, the legacy will fail, i.e. it will be adeemed.

Administration Bond: This is a special document required by the Probate Office when a deceased dies intestate. The bond must be executed by the administrator(s) and normally by an insurance company which guarantees to pay up to double the gross assets of the estate in the event of the estate being dissipated by the administrator(s).

Administrator/Adminstratrix: An administrator or administratrix (female) is the person or persons appointed to administer an estate when an individual has died intestate or without appointing an executor.

Advance Directives/Living Wills: It is possible for persons to set out their views with regard to future medical care, by way of what are known as Advance Directives (also known as Living Wills).

Affidavit: This is a statement in writing made on oath before a commissioner for oaths or a practising solicitor.

Approved Minimum Retirement Fund (AMRF): If the pensioner does not have the minimum of £10,000 annual income, he/she will be required to place £50,000 of the personal pension fund into an Approved Minimum Retirement Fund (AMRF) which cannot fall below £50,000 until the pensioner reaches the age of 75, after which it can be drawn out.

Approved Retirement Fund (ARF): If the pensioner has a guaranteed income for life of £10,000 through pension or annuity, his/her personal pension fund can be transferred to an Approved Retirement Fund (ARF) which is managed by a bank, building society, credit union or insurance company.

Barring Order: A court may prohibit the other spouse from leaving, calling to, or being present at the family home of the applicant/spouse.

Beneficiary: A beneficiary is a person who receives any legacy, bequest or devise under a will or where a person dies intestate.

Bequest: A bequest is normally a gift of a specific item of property, e.g. an item of furniture or a painting, to a beneficiary under a will.

Bereavement Grant: A bereavement grant of £500 applies in respect of persons who died on or after 2 February 1999. This is subject to certain requirements.

Codicil: A codicil is an addition, subtraction or explanation of a will. It is made by the testator subsequent to it, to become part of it and must be executed with the same formalities as a will.

Committee: If a person is made a ward of court, a committee of the person and a committee of the estate are appointed by the court. The committee of the person is similar to a guardian and has a duty to look after the physical welfare of the ward. The committee of the estate is similar to a trustee and can make representations to the wards of court office regarding the ward's property and investments. Normally the same individuals are appointed committee of the person and committee of the estate.

Contingent Benefit: This is a Pension Adjustment Order where the court directs a pension benefit to be paid under a pension scheme on the death of the member spouse while still in employment, to the non-member spouse.

D.I.R.T. Tax: Deposit Interest Retention Tax (D.I.R.T.) is payable on ordinary deposit accounts at 24 per cent and at 20 per cent on special savings accounts for the year ended 5 April 2000.

Deed of Covenant: A person may covenant to make annual payments to a beneficiary for a minimum period whereby his own total income for tax purposes is reduced and the beneficiary's income is thereby increased.

Deed of Separation: A Deed of Separation is an agreement in the form of a written contract entered into between a married couple, that sets out the agreed terms on which the couple will separate.

Defined Benefit Scheme: This is an occupational pension scheme which clearly sets out in the rules, the members' entitlements on retirement in these schemes. It is common for the scheme to grant one-sixtieth of the final salary for each year of service.

Defined Contribution Scheme: This is an occupational pension scheme in which the employer and the members contribute to the scheme at an agreed fixed rate. In these schemes, the member's benefits on retirement will depend on the total amount contributed to the fund and the investment returns earned.

Dependent Child Allowance: If you have children who are residing with you and who are financially dependent on you, you may claim Dependent Child Allowance as an additional sum. This is paid each week with your State pension.

Devise: A devise is generally the gift of a house or land to a beneficiary under a will.

Discretionary Trust: A discretionary trust gives discretion to the trustees as to how much of the trust fund is distributed, i.e. whether there is a capital sum distributed or whether or all or part of the income from the capital is distributed to one or more beneficiaries.

Enduring Power of Attorney (EPA): An enduring power of attorney is a power of attorney which can only be operated if the donor (the person who creates the document) becomes mentally incapable of managing his/her affairs.

Equities: This is the term used for shares traded on the Stock Exchange.

Equity Release Plan: This is where a person may transfer their interest in a property in return for a regular income.

Executor/Executrix: An executor or an executrix (female) is the person or persons named in the will to carry out the wishes of the deceased expressed in the will.

Exempt Approved Pension Schemes: These are pension schemes which are approved, or are in the process of seeking approval, or which are statutory schemes under the appropriate provisions of the Finance Act 1972 as amended by part 30 of the Taxes Consolidation Act 1997.

Express Trust: This is the most common form of trust. In an express trust, the subject matter, i.e. monies or property, and the objects, i.e. the beneficiaries of the trust, are clearly expressed.

Financial Compensation Order: In a divorce hearing, a court may order that on the death of one spouse, the proceeds of the life policy or pension benefit will be paid to the other spouse.

Gilts: This is the term used for government stocks/bonds traded on the Stock Exchange.

Grant of Representation: A Grant of Representation refers to either a Grant of Probate or Letters of Administration which issues from the High Court Probate Office to an executor or administrator on the death of a testator or intestate.

Guaranteed Growth Bonds: Guaranteed growth bonds are similar to income bonds except that the interest accumulated is paid out to you at the end of the term, together with the original investment.

Guaranteed Income Bonds: This is an investment where a lump sum is invested for a fixed term, usually three, four or five years. At the end of the term the original investment is returned. During the term you can receive a guaranteed tax paid income.

Guardian: A guardian is a person appointed under a will to take over the deceased's role as parent in rearing the deceased's children who are under the age of eighteen years of age.

Inheritance Tax: Inheritance tax is a tax which must be paid by a beneficiary under a will or on intestacy if the beneficiary receives a benefit which exceeds that beneficiary's inheritance tax free threshold.

Inland Revenue Affidavit: This is the document which sets out all the assets and liabilities of the deceased at the date of death, which are located in Ireland or abroad. It is sworn by the executor or administrator and sent to the Revenue Commissioners with any probate tax payable.

Inquiry Order: This is an order made by a High Court judge, confirming that there is sufficient medical evidence to consider making a person a ward of court.

Intestate: This is a person who has died without leaving a valid will or who has not, in a valid will, disposed of all his/her property.

Investment Bonds: These consist of property bonds, equity bonds, fixed interest (gilt), cash bonds, international equity bonds, managed bonds etc.

Joint Tenancy: This is a form of joint ownership of property where the surviving owner will automatically inherit the share of a deceased owner on that person's death.

Jointly and Severally: Attorneys under a power of attorney may be appointed to act jointly and severally, i.e. they may act either together or separately from each other.

Judicial Separation: If a couple cannot agree on a Deed of Separation between them and cannot or do not wish to apply for a divorce, then they can apply for a judicial separation in the courts.

Legacy: A legacy is usually a gift of money to a beneficiary under a will.

Legal Right Share: Under the Succession Act 1965, a surviving spouse is legally entitled to a share of the estate of a deceased spouse. The specific amount depends on whether the deceased had any children. This right is called a legal right share.

Letter of Wishes: This is a letter by the testator/testatrix, giving guidelines to the trustees named in a will as to how they might operate a trust for the benefit of the beneficiaries named.

Letters of Administration: This is the authority given to a person, the administrator or administratrix, by the High Court under its seal, to realise the estate of a deceased person where the deceased died intestate, i.e. without a will or where no executor has been named in a valid will.

Maintenance Pending Suit Order: Once proceedings have been issued for a Decree of Divorce/Judicial Separation, it is possible for one of the parties to apply for maintenance until the court application is heard.

Means Test: Your means or any income you or your spouse/partner have, or property (except your home), or other asset which could provide you with an income which exceeds £6 per week, is means tested.

Normal Pensionable Age: The rules of pension schemes generally stipulate that pensions are to be paid from a specified date. In most occupations this can be any age between 60 and 70, the most common age being 65.

Oath of Administrator: This is the document sworn by administrators, whereby they undertake to pay all the debts and liabilities of the deceased and distribute the estate among the beneficiaries as set out in the Succession Act 1965.

Oath of Executor: This is an affidavit sworn by the executors, whereby they undertake to pay all the debts and liabilities of the deceased and to discharge all the bequests and legacies contained in the will.

Occupational Pension Scheme: This is any scheme or arrangement which is: a) comprised of one or more instruments or agreements, and b) which provides benefits, or is capable of providing benefits, in relation to employees in any description of employment who reside within the State and meet other requirements.

Old Age Contributory Pension: This is paid to persons who reach the age of 66 and who have paid the necessary PRSI contributions before reaching the age of 56.

Old Age Non-Contributory Pension: You will qualify for an Old Age Non-Contributory Pension is you are aged 66 or over and you are living in the State and satisfy a means test.

Pension Adjustment Order: This is where a court directs a portion of a pension fund to be transferred to the non-member spouse, in the form of a retirement benefit.

Pension Schemes: Pension schemes provide for a tax effective means of saving for retirement, i.e. contributions to the pension scheme qualify for tax relief subject to limits and no tax is paid on the income or gains of the pension scheme.

Periodical Payments Order: On the granting of divorce/judicial separation, the court may make a periodical payments order, directing a spouse to make payments to the other spouse, for that spouse's support.

Personal Equity Plan (PEP): PEPs are funds that are invested entirely in equities (shares), usually with a sufficient portion in Irish shares to qualify for a lower rate of tax (20 per cent).

Personal Investment Plan (PIP): PIPs are invested in managed unit funds with a reasonably broad mix of Government unit bonds, shares and cash.

Personal Pensions: These are normally availed of by many self-employed people and the pension fund on retirement depends on the number and the amount of contributions made as well as profits from the investment.

Personal Representative: The personal representative is the term used to describe an executor or administrator of a deceased person who is responsible for administering the deceased's estate.

Power of Attorney: A power of attorney is a legal arrangement whereby one person (the donor) gives authority to another or others (the attorney/s) to act on his/her behalf.

Probate: This is the document which issues to the executor from the Probate Office bearing the seal of the High Court. It authorises the executor to act in the administration of the estate and has an authenticated copy of the will attached.

Probate Tax: This is a 2 per cent tax, which must be paid on the value of all property of a deceased person, exceeding £40,000 in value, after 1 December 1999, other than joint property, monies paid under a superannuation scheme, or anything inherited by a surviving spouse.

Protection Order: A court may order that a spouse is to refrain from molesting, frightening, or using or threatening to use violence against the applicant or the dependent person.

PRSI Contributions: All employees whether full-time or part-time and self-employed workers with an income of £2,500 per year or more, are liable for Pay Related Social Insurance (PRSI) contributions. These are used to help pay for social welfare benefits and pensions.

Qualified Adult Allowance: If your spouse (or cohabiting partner) does not have an income of £60 or more per week, you are entitled to claim a Qualified Adult Allowance in respect of him/her, if he/she is dependent on you.

Retirement Pension: You will qualify for a State retirement pension if you are aged 65, or retired from full-time employment, or if you satisfy certain PRSI contribution conditions.

Settlement: A trust created by a will or a declaration of trust made during the settlor's lifetime is called a settlement.

Settlor: A settlor is a person who creates a trust.

State Pensions: These consist of Contributory or Non-Contributory Old Age pensions.

Statement of Facts: This is an affidavit sworn by the applicant in wardship proceedings which sets out a number of matters including who should be appointed committee of the ward and makes suggestions as to what is to happen with the ward's property.

Substituted Judgement: This is where the court puts itself in the place of an incompetent patient and decides what the patient would have wished in the particular circumstances regarding what medical treatment should be carried out.

Subvention: A subvention is normally made by a local health board to help to pay for the cost of maintenance in a nursing home, when certain conditions are met.

Supplementary Welfare Allowance (SWA): This is an additional health board payment payable to people receiving social welfare benefits who are on a very low income or have insufficient means.

Surety: A guarantor is a person who binds himself/herself by deed to satisfy the obligations of another person if the latter fails to do so. A surety to an administration bond must swear a justification of surety that he/she is worth a sum equal to the gross assets in the deceased's estate.

Target Pension: Defined contribution schemes often give members a quotation, which is a "target pension". This is to give members an idea of what pensions they can expect on retirement.

Tax Allowance: A tax allowance is a deduction from gross income for income tax purposes.

Tax Credit: A tax credit is a deduction from a tax liability for income tax purposes.

Tenancy in Common: This a form of co-ownership whereby two or more persons have an undivided beneficial interest in property giving them possession of it, none of them having exclusive possession of the whole of any part. Unlike a joint tenancy, the interest of a tenant in common does not pass automatically on his death to the other co-owners.

Testator/Testatrix: This is the person who makes his/her will.

Tracker Bonds: Tracker bonds are usually set up as either deposits or life insurance policies. They provide a return based on the growth in the Stock Market index or basket of Stock Market indices.

Trust: A trust is a document created by a person called the settlor. The settlor by will or deed appoints a trustee or trustees to carry out the terms of the trust and in whom ownership of the trust property is vested until the trust property is transferred to the beneficiaries, i.e. the objects of the trust.

Trustee: The trustees are appointed in a will or deed to carry out the terms of the trust and to hold the trust property for the benefit of beneficiaries until the beneficiaries reach a specific age, or for their lifetime, whichever is stipulated by the trust.

Unit Trusts: Unit trusts are probably the simplest way of investing in the Stock Market and involve a group of investors, a fund manager and a trustee.

Unit-linked Bonds: A unit-linked bond is very similar to a unit trust. The difference is that the unit-linked fund has a life assurance policy attached to it and does not have trustees.

Unit-Linked Funds: A unit-linked bond/fund is an open-ended investment which you can cash in at any stage. Your lump sum is used to buy units in one or more of a range of investment bonds.

Ward of Court: A ward of court is a person who is declared to be of unsound mind and incapable of managing his/her person or property, i.e. the person cannot look after himself/herself physically and cannot manage finances.

Will : A will is a written document in which a person sets out legally binding wishes in relation to the distribution of property after a death.

Index

additional voluntary contributions (AVCs) 55
advance directives 161-3
age allowance 120-1
agents 27-8, 32-3, 129
assets, outside Ireland 27-8
attorneys 34-6, 42-3
AVCs (additional voluntary contributions) 55

bank accounts, joint 27, 31-2
bereavement allowance 122
bereavement grant 74-5
blind pension 77
blind person's allowance 77, 122
blind welfare allowance 77
bonds 114-16
Business Expansion Scheme 117

capital acquisitions tax 11-12
capital gains tax 25, 129-34
carers 75, 76-7, 122-3
carer's allowance 75, 76-7, 122-3
charitable bequests 26
child benefits 89
children
divorce/separation and 146
wills 6-7, 28
Civic Legal Aid Scheme 168-9
community care services 95-6
community social workers 95
community support schemes 85-6
court jurisdiction, divorce/separation and 152
covenants 49-50, 105
Credit Unions 110
creditors, statutory notice to 28

day centres 96

death
capital gains tax 133
funeral arrangements 17
payments arising from 74-5
deferred annuities 132
defined benefit pension schemes 54
defined contribution pensions schemes 54
Department of Enterprise, Trade and Development 171
dependent relatives allowance 105, 121
deposit accounts 109
disabled drivers 78
disabled passengers 78
DIRT tax 109, 110, 128-9
disability allowance 76
disability benefit 76
divorce 5, 145-52
domestic violence 151
domicile, capital acquisitions tax and 12
drivers, disabled 78
drugs payment scheme 85

Eastern Regional Health Authority 100
electricity, free 80-81
enduring powers of attorney 36-42
equity investments 112-13
estate, administration of 29
EU farm retirement scheme 71-2
executors 4, 18-20, 22

family compensation orders 149-50
family home, divorce/separation and 149
family home relief 11-12
film industry investment 117
financial support for older people 61-3
forestry funds 117

free bottled gas 82
free electricity 80-81, 82-3
free natural gas 81-2
free schemes 78
free telephone 83-4
free travel 78-80
fuel allowance 84
funded occupational pensions 53
funeral arrangements 17

gas, free 81-2
gift tax 12-16
government stocks/bonds 112
grant of probate 21, 24-5
guardians 5

health board nursing homes 96-7
health expenses 124-5
health insurance 123
home carer's allowance 75, 76-7,
    122-3
home helps 95
home reversion 106
hospices 97

incapacitated child allowance 121
income tax
grant of probate and 24
married couples 118-19
PAYE 119
personal allowance rates 119-20, 138-
    41
residents 118
unmarried couples 119
indexation relief 129
Information Commissioner 166-8
inheritance tax 12-16, 25
Inland Revenue affidavit 21-2
insurance information service
    171
Insurance Ombudsman 169-71
invalidity pension   76
investment funds   113-17
investments 108-12

joint bank accounts 27, 31-2
joint property, wills and 7-8
judicial separation 144-52

legal fees, for administration of estate
    29-30
legal separation, wills and 5
letter of wishes 8
letters of administration 23-4
life assurance policies 132
living wills 161-3

maintenance 146-8
managed funds 113
marital breakdown 142 *see also*
        divorce; separation
married couples, capital gains tax 129-
    30
meals on wheels 96
medical card 84-5
medical treatment, consent 157-9
mobility allowance 77-8
mortgage assistance 76
mortgage interest   income tax 126
mutual funds 116

National Investment Savings 111
nursing homes 97-105

occupational pensions 52-7
old age contributory pension 64-7
old age non-contributory pensions 67-
    70
ombudsman 165-6
one parent tax allowance 121-2

passengers, disabled 78
PAYE allowance 120
payment orders 148-9
pension adjustment orders 150
pension contributions, income tax and
    125
pensions 51-9, 63-70, 73-4, 76, 125
Pensions Board 59
PEPs (personal equity plans) 113
permanent health benefit 123-4
personal equity plans (PEPs) 113
personal investment plans (PIPs) 114
personal pensions 57-9
personal representatives 17-18
PIPs 114
Post Office schemes 110-11

powers of attorney 34-42
Powers of Attorney Act 1996 37, 38-9
pre-retirement allowance 71
principal private residence, capital
    gains tax 130
private nursing homes 96
private rented accommodation, income
    tax 125
probate tax 9-11
property funds 114
providing for spouse out of estate 151
PRSI contributions 61-2
public health nursing 95

rates
capital gains tax 130
personal allowances 119-20, 138-41
redundancy, lump sum payments
    127-8
registration, of enduring power of
    attorney 41-2
rent assistance 76
residential care 96, 105-6
retirement
lump sum payments 127-8
pension 63-4
relief 132
Revenue Commissioners, complaining
    to 129
rollover relief 132
RSI number 118

savings, introduction 108-12
Savings Bonds 111
Savings Certificates 111
self-employed pensions 66-7
separation 5, 143-52

service charges, tax relief 126
sickness benefit 76
small claims court 164-5
social assistance rates 88-9
social information leaflets 87
social insurance rates 87-8
social welfare legislation 26-7
social welfare payments 32-3, 61
solicitors 2, 153
Special Savings Accounts 109-10
standard capital superannuation benefit
    128
supplementary welfare payments 75-8
surviving spouse, rights of 25-6

tangible movable assets 131-2
tax free allowance   120
tax offices 136-7
tax provisions, divorce/separation and
    152
telephone, free 83-4
testator 1
testatrix 1
tracker bonds 114-15
travel pass 61
trustees 4, 20-21
trusts 47-9

unit linked bonds 116
unit trusts 116

voluntary nursing homes 96

wards of court43-7, 159-61
wardship 43-7
widows/widowers, pensions 73-4
wills 1-9, 161-3

EUGENE F. COLLINS

SOLICITORS

Temple Chambers,
3, Burlington Road,
Dublin 4.
D.X. 25

Tel: +353 1 667 5111
Fax: +353 1 667 5200
E-Mail: lawyer@efc.ie
Website: http//www.efc.ie

Corporate / Commercial
Contact: Gerard Coll

Insolvency
Contact: Barry O'Neill

Litigation
Contact: Terry Leggett

Intellectual Property
Contact: Eugene Murphy

Property Law
Contact: David Ensor

Employment Law
Contact: Simon McCormick

Private Client / Trusts / Estate Planning
Contact: John Costello